Surviving the Wild

Essential First Aid and Emergency Techniques

By
Well-Being Publishing

Copyright 2023 Well-Being Publishing. All rights reserved.

No part of this book may be reproduced in any form or by any electronic or mechanical means including information storage and retrieval systems, without permission in writing from the author. The only exception is by a reviewer, who may quote short excerpts in a review.

Although the author and publisher have made every effort to ensure that the information in this book was correct at press time, the author and publisher do not assume and hereby disclaim any liability to any party for any loss, damage, or disruption caused by errors or omissions, whether such errors or omissions result from negligence, accident, or any other cause.

This publication is designed to provide accurate and authoritative information with regard to the subject matter covered. It is sold with the understanding that the publisher is not engaged in rendering professional services. If legal advice or other expert assistance is required, the services of a competent professional should be sought.

The fact that an organization or website is referred to in this work as a citation and/or a potential source of further information does not mean that the author or the publisher endorses the information the organization or website may provide or recommendations it may make.

Please remember that Internet websites listed in this work may have changed or disappeared between when this work was written and when it is read.

To You,

Thank You!

Table of Contents

Chapter 1: Surviving the Wild: Essential First Aid | and Emergency Techniques 1

Introduction 4

Chapter 2: Understanding Wilderness First Aid 8
    The Basics of Wilderness Medicine 8
    Wilderness First Aid VS. Urban First Aid 9
    Preparing a Wilderness First Aid Kit 12
    Essentials for Your Kit 12

Chapter 3: Principles of Emergency Management 16
    Assessing an Emergency 17
    Primary and Secondary Assessments 17
    Calling for Help in the Wild 20
    When and How to Signal for Assistance 21

Chapter 4: Responding to Environmental Hazards 25
    Heat-Related Illnesses 25
    Recognition and Treatment 26
    Cold-Related Injuries 29
    Hypothermia and Frostbite Management 30
    Altitude Sickness 33
    Prevention and Care 33

Chapter 5: Handling Bites and Stings 37
    Snake Bites 38
    First Aid Steps 38
    Insect Bites and Stings 41

Treatment and Prevention 42
Animal Attacks 45
Immediate Response Tactics... 45

Chapter 6: Wound Care in the Wilderness 49
Cleaning and Dressing Wounds.. 50
Techniques and Tips 50
Managing Bleeding 53
Direct Pressure and Tourniquets 54
Shock 57
Recognition and Initial Care... 57

Chapter 7: Fractures and Sprains... 61
Splinting Techniques... 62
Improvised and Commercial Splints 62
Managing Sprains and Strains 65
RICE Technique (Rest, Ice, Compression, Elevation).................... 65

Chapter 8: Water Safety and Drowning Prevention 69
Recognizing Drowning 69
Signs and Symptoms of Drowning 70
Rescue Techniques 73
Safe Rescue and Initial Care... 74

Chapter 9: Wilderness Survival Skills 77
Building Shelters 77
Types and Techniques... 78
Finding Water and Food... 81
Safe Sources and Preparation 82

Chapter 10: Navigating Common Health Issues 86
Dealing with Allergies... 86
EpiPen Usage... 87
Managing Chronic Conditions in the Wilderness 90
Diabetes, Asthma, and Others.. 91

Chapter 11: Advanced First Aid Techniques 95
   Performing CPR 96
   Guidelines and Steps: Performing CPR 97
   Using an Automated External Defibrillator (AED) 100
   Operation and Safety 100

Chapter 12: Mental Health and Crisis Management 104
   Dealing with Panic and Anxiety 104
   Techniques for Calming and Support 105
   Recognizing and Addressing PTSD in Survival Situations 108
   Support Strategies 109

Chapter 13: Legal and Ethical Considerations 112
   Understanding Your Legal Obligations 112
   Good Samaritan Laws 113
   Ethical Dilemmas in Wilderness First Aid 116
   Decision Making in Emergency Situations 117
   This Book Review Request 120

Conclusion 121

Appendix A: Appendix 125
   Wilderness First Aid Checklist 125
   Emergency Communication Planning 126
   Recommended Reading and Resources 126
   Wilderness First Aid Checklist 127
   Emergency Communication Planning 130
   Recommended Reading and Resources 133

Chapter 1:
Surviving the Wild: Essential First Aid and Emergency Techniques

The great outdoors offers an escape, an adventure, and a test of our limits. However, it's also a place where preparation meets the unpredictability of nature head-on. Knowing how to handle an emergency situation, provide first aid, and possibly save a life becomes paramount. This chapter dives into the essential first aid and emergency techniques that can make the difference between a story of survival and a cautionary tale.

First and foremost, understanding the basics of wilderness first aid is not just about memorizing procedures; it's about developing a mindset geared towards prevention, assessment, and immediate action. Before you even pack your gear, cultivating the knowledge and skills for emergencies is akin to packing an invisible survival kit—one that could be more crucial than any tool in your backpack.

One of the foundational aspects of wilderness first aid is learning to quickly assess an emergency situation. Time and resources are limited in the wild, making it vital to understand the priority of care. Prioritization can mean the difference between a manageable situation and one that spirals out of control.

Communication plays a key role in emergency scenarios. In the wilderness, where cell service may be nonexistent, knowing how to signal for help becomes an essential skill. Techniques such as using mirrors, creating smoke signals, or employing a whistle can mean the difference between being found or remaining lost.

Environmental hazards present some of the most immediate threats to safety in the wild. Recognizing the signs of heat stroke, hypothermia, or altitude sickness early on can prevent a minor issue from becoming a severe problem. The knowledge of how to mitigate these risks through adaptation and immediate care is crucial.

Encounters with wildlife, from insect bites to potentially dangerous animal interactions, pose significant risks. Understanding how to prevent such encounters and respond effectively if they occur will enhance your safety. This includes knowing the specifics of first aid treatment for various bites and stings, which can significantly reduce complications.

Wounds received in the wilderness require special attention due to the higher risk of infection and complications. Learning the proper techniques for cleaning and dressing wounds, managing bleeding, and recognizing signs of shock are skills that can save a limb or even a life.

One of the more common injuries includes fractures and sprains. Knowing how to properly splint an injury or manage a sprain using the RICE technique (Rest, Ice, Compression, Elevation) will help stabilize an injured individual until professional help can be reached.

Water safety is another critical area, especially for adventurers who find themselves near or in bodies of water. Recognizing the signs of drowning and knowing safe rescue techniques can prevent tragedies. This knowledge couples with an understanding of how to perform CPR and possibly use an automated external defibrillator (AED), which are invaluable skills in critical moments.

Wilderness survival isn't just about dealing with immediate physical threats; it also involves managing chronic conditions under challenging circumstances. For individuals with conditions such as diabetes or asthma, knowing how to manage these effectively in the wild is as crucial as any emergency procedure.

Mental health is equally as important as physical health in crisis situations. The ability to stay calm, make calculated decisions, and possibly support others who are dealing with panic or anxiety can prevent a situation from worsening. The strength of the mind is a powerful ally in survival scenarios.

While this chapter provides an overview and foundational knowledge, remember that practical application through courses, hands-on practice, and continuous learning is essential. Skills need to be honed, and knowledge kept fresh through repeated practice and update of information.

The wilderness calls to many as a place of beauty and adventure. A respect for its power and unpredictability should always accompany that call. Preparedness, knowledge, and the right attitude towards safety can ensure that your outdoor adventures are memorable for all the right reasons. Remember, survival in the wild begins long before you set foot in it; it starts with the knowledge and skills you've chosen to arm yourself with.

As you continue through this book, each chapter will build upon the next, creating a comprehensive guide designed to equip you with the skills necessary for a safe and fulfilling wilderness experience. Let the journey begin.

In the following chapters, we'll delve deeper into each of these areas, providing detailed explanations, guidelines, and practical tips to ensure you're prepared for whatever the wild throws your way. The goal is not just to survive but to thrive, respecting nature's boundaries while embracing the adventures she offers.

Introduction

Embarking on an adventure into the wilderness ignites a sense of freedom and connection with nature that is unmatched. Whether you're scaling remote mountains, traversing vast forests, or exploring untouched landscapes, the call of the wild is irresistible to outdoor enthusiasts, adventurers, campers, and hikers alike. Yet, with this exhilarating exploration comes the undeniable fact that the wilderness is unforgiving. The very essence that makes it wildly beautiful - its unpredictability and remoteness - can turn any adventure into a survival situation in the blink of an eye. This is where the knowledge and skills of wilderness first aid and emergency care become not just advantageous, but essential.

Embarking on the journey of mastering wilderness first aid is much more than learning a set of skills; it's about adopting a mindset that prepares you for the unexpected. It's about becoming a resilient and resourceful individual who can confidently face challenges and make crucial decisions under pressure. The goal of this book is to empower you with the comprehensive knowledge and practical skills necessary to effectively manage injuries, respond to emergencies, and provide lifesaving care in wilderness settings.

Wilderness first aid is a unique discipline that extends beyond the confines of traditional first aid. It is tailored for scenarios where help is not immediately available, where medical resources are limited, and where environmental factors compound the severity of every crisis. Unlike urban settings, where professional medical assistance may be moments away, wilderness scenarios require you to rely on your own capabilities to stabilize and care for the injured until further help can be secured.

The journey we're about to embark on together will not only cover the practicalities of handling common injuries and emergencies in the wild but also the psychological aspects of providing care in high-stress situations. You'll learn how to remain calm and effective when faced with adversity, how to prioritize tasks in an emergency, and how to use the tools and resources at your disposal creatively.

As we step into this adventure together, it's important to recognize that the wilderness does not discriminate. It presents challenges to novice hikers and seasoned outdoor professionals alike. Whether you're planning a day trip or a lengthy expedition, being prepared with advanced first aid knowledge can mean the difference between life and death. This book is designed not merely as a manual but as a companion for your journey, offering guidance, inspiration, and practical advice to ensure your time in the wild is safe and fulfilling.

Throughout this book, we will cover a wide range of topics essential for a well-rounded understanding of wilderness first aid. From preparing a comprehensive first aid kit tailored for wilderness adventures, managing environmental hazards, to handling bites, stings, and injuries specific to remote settings - every chapter is crafted to enrich your knowledge and enhance your readiness.

Moreover, we delve into principles of emergency management, teaching you how to assess emergencies, perform primary and secondary assessments, and initiate the appropriate response. Recognizing the importance of being able to call for help in the wilderness, we include guidance on effectively signaling for assistance, a crucial skill in remote areas.

Our exploration will not shy away from the daunting aspects of wilderness first aid, such as managing severe bleeding, recognizing and treating shock, and addressing fractures and sprains with improvised means. We'll also tackle the critical topics of water safety, drowning prevention, and the basics of survival skills, like building shelters and finding water.

Navigating common health issues in the wilderness, such as allergies and chronic conditions, is also paramount. Preparedness in these aspects can significantly impact the outcome of your wilderness adventures. Advanced techniques, including CPR and the use of an Automated External Defibrillator (AED), will be demystified, ensuring you're equipped with the knowledge to perform these potentially lifesaving procedures.

Understanding the psychological challenges that can arise in wilderness settings is equally important. We'll discuss strategies for managing panic and anxiety, recognizing and addressing post-traumatic stress disorder (PTSD) in survival situations, and providing support to others facing mental health challenges in these environments.

Lastly, we'll delve into the legal and ethical considerations of providing first aid in the wilderness. Understanding your legal obligations and the ethical dilemmas you may face is crucial for anyone taking on the responsibility of caring for others in remote settings.

This book is more than a guide; it's an invitation to embrace the unpredictability of the wilderness with confidence. It's about equipping yourself with the knowledge and skills to face whatever challenges might arise, knowing that you are prepared. It's about becoming a guardian for yourself and others, ensuring that every adventure is as safe as it is thrilling.

So, let us embark on this journey together, with open minds and eager hearts, ready to learn and grow. The skills and knowledge you acquire through these pages will not only serve you in the wild; they will empower you in every aspect of your life, fostering resilience, confidence, and a deep-rooted sense of preparedness that transcends beyond the wilderness.

Welcome to your first step toward mastering wilderness first aid and emergency care. Together, we will unlock the full potential of your outdoor adventures, ensuring they are memorable for their beauty and excitement, not the emergencies that we have prepared to overcome.

Chapter 2:
Understanding Wilderness First Aid

As we transition from the foundational skills discussed earlier, we delve into the heart of wilderness first aid, a realm where preparation meets action. Unlike its urban counterpart, wilderness first aid is the art of improvisation; learning to make do with what you have while being miles away from professional help. It's about understanding not just the 'how' but the 'why' behind each technique and decision. Within this chapter, you'll explore the critical differences between wilderness and urban first aid, underscoring the unique challenges and creative solutions required when you're off the beaten path. Preparing a wilderness first aid kit transforms from a simple task to a thoughtful exercise in anticipation—each item selected with purpose and foresight. You'll learn that beyond bandages and antiseptics, your first aid kit must include knowledge, confidence, and the readiness to act. Embracing wilderness first aid is a journey towards self-reliance and resilience, empowering you to protect not only yourself but also those who venture with you. As we unpack the layers of wilderness medicine and kit essentials, remember that each chapter is a step further into becoming the calm in the storm, equipped with the skills to navigate the unpredictable nature of outdoor adventures with grace and competence.

The Basics of Wilderness Medicine

In the realm of outdoor adventures, understanding the basics of wilderness medicine is vital for anyone stepping off the beaten path.

This knowledge is the foundation upon which the safety and well-being of both yourself and your fellow explorers rest. Unlike conventional medical care, wilderness medicine focuses on pre-hospital, remote settings where immediate medical help is not readily available. It's about making do with what you have on hand, improvising solutions, and decisively acting to prevent situations from worsening. By embracing these principles, you can transform uncertainty into confidence, fear into action. It's not merely about treating injuries or illnesses; it's about preventing them where possible and ensuring everyone in your party has the knowledge and skills to help each other. As you delve deeper into this section, keep in mind that every technique and bit of knowledge acquired is a step toward becoming a more competent, self-reliant, and inspiring figure in the wild. Let the journey begin.

Wilderness First Aid VS. Urban First Aid

When venturing into the world of first aid, it's essential to recognize the nuanced differences between wilderness first aid and its urban counterpart. Both are critical in their contexts, yet they operate under different assumptions, protocols, and sometimes, objectives.

In urban settings, professional medical help is often just minutes away. An ambulance can be at your doorstep rapidly, equipped with lifesaving equipment and trained personnel. Thus, urban first aid often focuses on stabilizing the patient for a short duration until professional help arrives.

Conversely, wilderness first aid operates under the "golden hour" principle, which is extended significantly due to remote locations. Assistance may be hours or even days away, compelling the responder to provide not just immediate care but also prolonged support under potentially harsh environmental conditions.

The tools and resources available in each setting also diverge significantly. Urban environments typically offer easy access to advanced medical kits, whereas wilderness responders must make do with what's on hand or what they've brought with them, emphasizing the importance of a well-thought-out wilderness first aid kit.

Moreover, the nature of injuries encountered can differ. Urban first aid often deals with issues like car accidents or domestic injuries, which are less likely in the wilderness. In contrast, wilderness injuries might include exposure-related conditions, wildlife interactions, and trauma from falls or navigation mishaps.

One of the critical skills in wilderness first aid is improvisation. Urban environments provide the luxury of specialized equipment, but in the wild, a first aider might need to fashion splints from branches or create stretchers from hiking poles and clothing. This creativity can make a significant difference in patient outcomes.

Preparation and prevention are emphasized much more in wilderness first aid. Understanding the environment you're entering, knowing potential hazards, and being prepared with both knowledge and supplies to mitigate these risks is half the battle won.

Communication challenges are also a stark distinguishing factor. In urban scenarios, help is a phone call away, but in remote areas, first responders may need to employ specialized devices like satellite phones or emergency beacons to call for help, and even then, help might not be immediate.

Training for these two types of first aid also differs. Urban first aid courses often focus on scenarios and resources common to city settings. Wilderness first aid training, meanwhile, delves into remote care principles, long-term patient management, and environment-specific risks and responses.

The psychological aspect of providing care in isolated settings cannot be understated. Wilderness first aid may require staying calm and making critical decisions in intimidating, sometimes life-threatening situations without backup. This mental resilience is key to effective wilderness first response.

Environmental conditions play a significant role in wilderness first aid. Weather can change swiftly, turning a relatively stable situation into a critical one. Understanding how to protect a patient, and oneself, from elements is an invaluable aspect of wilderness training.

It's also worth noting that the scope of care may expand in wilderness settings. First responders might need to address basic needs such as hydration, shelter, and warmth over extended periods, tasks less commonly associated with urban first aid.

Legally, the expectation and implications of providing first aid can differ based on location. Good Samaritan laws vary by jurisdiction, but remote settings might impose different expectations and obligations on a first responder, something wilderness first aid training often covers.

In conclusion, while the core principles of preserving life, preventing further harm, and promoting recovery remain constant, wilderness first aid is a unique beast. It demands a broader skill set, a higher degree of resourcefulness, and a mindset prepared for the unpredictability of nature. As much as it's about medical response, it's equally about adaptation, resilience, and overcoming challenges that the great outdoors presents. For adventurers, this knowledge isn't just beneficial; it's essential for the safety of oneself and others.

Embrace the journey of learning wilderness first aid. It's not merely about acquiring skills for emergency scenarios; it's a transformative process that equips you with confidence, knowledge, and the capacity to make a difference in critical moments. Your journey into the wild will be safer, and you will stand as a beacon of leadership and competence in the face of adversity.

Preparing a Wilderness First Aid Kit

Embarking into the wilderness requires not just courage and a spirit of adventure but also preparation and foresight, especially when it comes to health and safety. Preparing a wilderness first aid kit is a crucial step in this journey towards self-reliance and resilience. Think of your first aid kit as your trusty sidekick, equipped to handle the unexpected twists and turns of the wild. Inside this compact yet powerful tool, you'll carry items that address a wide range of scenarios—from minor cuts and abrasions to more serious conditions that require immediate attention before professional help can be reached. Essential components include various sizes of bandages, antiseptic wipes, adhesive tape, blister prevention supplies, gloves for infection control, tweezers, safety pins, a thermometer, and medications for common ailments like pain, fever, allergies, and stomach issues. Additionally, tools such as a multi-tool with scissors, a flashlight, and emergency blankets can be lifesavers in critical situations. Building your kit with thoughtfulness and intention isn't just about having the right items; it's about fostering a mindset of preparedness that empowers you to tackle challenges head-on, ensuring that you're ready to provide care in the wilderness with confidence and competence. Remember, in the great outdoors, where nature calls the shots, your wilderness first aid kit is your first line of defense in safeguarding your greatest adventure asset—your health.

Essentials for Your Kit

As we continue on our journey to mastering the art of wilderness survival and first aid, we've now arrived at a pivotal moment: constructing our wilderness first aid kit. This isn't just any kit; it's your frontline defense, your partner in the wild, and at times, it could very well mean the difference between life and death. Let's dive into the essentials you'll need, tailored specifically for the unpredictability and sheer vastness of the wilderness.

First and foremost, your kit must include items for wound management. This encompasses a variety of bandages, from adhesive bandages for minor cuts to sterile gauze pads for larger wound coverage. Antiseptic wipes and antibiotic ointment are also crucial to prevent infection. Remember, in the wilderness, preventing infection is not just advisable, it's imperative.

Next, tools for managing bleeding are essential. This means having a tourniquet, a necessity for controlling life-threatening bleeding, and hemostatic agents that can assist in clotting. However, these tools are not just items in your kit; they represent knowledge you must have. Knowing when and how to apply a tourniquet correctly is as vital as the item itself.

Fractures and sprains can occur easily in rugged outdoor environments, making it essential to include splints or even a SAM splint in your kit. Elastic bandages or wraps come in handy for strains and sprains, aiding in compression and support. The ability to immobilize an injury can prevent further damage and facilitate a safer extraction if necessary.

Environmental challenges like hypothermia or hyperthermia require special attention in your wilderness first aid kit. Items such as emergency blankets, which can reflect body heat back to the individual, are lightweight but lifesaving additions to your pack.

For those venturing into areas where snake bites or insect stings are a risk, incorporating specific supplies like an extraction pump or antihistamines could be crucial. However, the true essence of preparedness lies in education. Understanding the types of wildlife in your area and knowing the appropriate first-aid response is key.

Navigation tools might not seem like a conventional choice for a first aid kit, but in the wilderness, knowing your location and being able to communicate it is pivotal. A compact, waterproof set of maps and a compass (even better, learning how to use them) can help you find your way to safety if you're lost or need to guide rescuers to your location.

Water purification tablets or a small, portable filter is another non-traditional but critical item. In scenarios where you are stranded or delayed, access to clean drinking water becomes a matter of health and survival. Dehydration can exacerbate almost any medical situation.

Communication devices, specifically designed for wilderness environments where cellular service is a myth, like a satellite phone or a personal locator beacon (PLB), should find a place in your kit. In moments of distress, these tools can send a lifeline to the outside world.

Don't overlook the necessity of a comprehensive first-aid manual. Knowledge is power, and in the wild, it can also be survival. A waterproof, pocket-sized manual could guide through procedures when memory fails or panic sets in.

Lighting is another critical component. A reliable, waterproof flashlight or headlamp can assist with nighttime injuries or simply navigating the dark. Remember, spare batteries or an alternative charging method, like solar, ensure that light is available when you need it most.

Personal medications should not be overlooked. If you or your companions require prescribed medications, ensuring an adequate supply within your kit is fundamental. This also includes an epinephrine auto-injector for severe allergic reactions, which can be life-threatening without immediate treatment.

For those venturing into extreme conditions or far off the beaten path, items for shelter building, such as a lightweight tarp or bivy sack, could prove invaluable. These supplies offer protection against the elements, critical in situations where you might be immobilized or when waiting for rescue.

All these items represent a foundation, but the true essence of your wilderness first aid kit is customization. Consider the specific risks associated with your adventure, the environment you'll be entering, and the length of your journey. It is this thoughtful preparation that transforms a standard first aid kit into a powerful tool tailored to your unique wilderness journey.

In building your kit, let motivation and inspiration guide you. The wilderness calls to those who are prepared to listen and respond with respect and knowledge. Your journey into the wild is a testament to the human spirit's resilience, adaptability, and enduring call to adventure. As you assemble your first aid kit, remember, it is more than just supplies and tools; it is your commitment to safety, preparedness, and the unwavering will to thrive in the face of nature's challenges.

Chapter 3: Principles of Emergency Management

Emerging victorious in the wild requires more than courage and strength; it demands a profound understanding of the principles of emergency management, a cornerstone for any outdoor adventurer or professional working in remote areas. In grappling with the unpredictable nature of wilderness settings, mastering the art of assessing emergencies quickly and efficiently sets the stage for successful outcomes. This chapter dives deep into the essential skills of conducting both primary and secondary assessments—an intricate dance of observation, decision-making, and action that could mean the difference between survival and tragedy. Knowing when and how to signal for assistance is not just about waving a flare or sending an SOS; it's a calculated strategy that involves understanding the landscape, weather conditions, and available resources. This knowledge equips individuals with the power to transform fear into action, turning what might seem like insurmountable obstacles into manageable challenges. As you traverse through this chapter, remember, the heart of effective emergency management lies in preparation, presence of mind, and the profound belief in one's ability to make a difference when it matters most. Each page is designed to build not just skills, but the confidence and wisdom needed to face the unknown with assurance and competence.

Assessing an Emergency

In the heart of an emergency, especially within the untamed wilderness, the initial moments can define the fine line between success and distress. Assessing an emergency is your crucial first step in navigating the unpredictable sea of wilderness first aid. With every breath you take and every move you make, observation is your best friend. It's about quickly but effectively evaluating the situation, understanding the severity, and determining if you're facing a sprained ankle or a life-threatening condition. This process is not just about having the skills but about harnessing the courage and calm within the storm to make informed decisions. It bridges the gap between knowledge and action, empowering you to put your emergency plans into motion with confidence. Whether you're dealing with injuries from a fall, an unexpected illness, or any other sudden health crisis, remember that your ability to assess the situation accurately can be the difference between a story of survival or a tale of caution. This section will not delve into the nitty-gritty of subsequent steps like primary and secondary assessments, which are covered later but focuses squarely on sizing up the emergency itself, ensuring you're equipped to take the next steps with assurance and agility.

Primary and Secondary Assessments

In the wake of an emergency, especially those occurring in the wilderness, the assessment process is your blueprint for action. It's the critical window where you categorize emergencies into immediate, urgent, and non-urgent, guiding your response efforts effectively. The primary assessment, often referred to as the initial check, focuses on life-threatening conditions. Its swift, systematic approach ensures you address the most critical needs first.

Starting with the primary assessment, the mnemonic 'ABCDE' guides your process: Airway, Breathing, Circulation, Disability,

Exposure/Environment. First, ensure the airway is clear. Is the person talking or coughing? That's a good sign; if not, immediate action is needed to clear the airway. Next, check for breathing. Look, listen, and feel for breaths. If they're breathing, assess the quality and rate. Following this, evaluate circulation. Look for major bleeding, checking pulses to ensure blood is flowing. Disability refers to assessing neurological function; a quick check can be asking them to squeeze your hand. Lastly, consider exposure or environment—protect them and yourself from environmental risks. Remember, this is not just about making a diagnosis but rather stabilizing their condition.

After you've conducted your primary assessment, it's paramount to communicate your findings if you're in a group or with another responder. Clarity can save lives, so make your communication as clear and concise as possible. This approach prevents confusion and ensures that everyone involved understands the immediate actions required and why they're necessary. In some cases, the situation may demand immediate evacuation; early recognition is key.

Moving to the secondary assessment, this is where you take a more detailed look once you've ensured the victim is not in immediate danger. Consider this the 'fine-tooth comb' approach, where you systematically check from head to toe, front to back. Look for anything you might have missed in the primary assessment. Ask questions: What happened? Do they feel pain anywhere? Can they move all their limbs? Do they remember the incident? All while monitoring any changes in their condition. This step is essential for gathering information that could be crucial for professional medical personnel later.

The SAMPLE history is a useful guide during the secondary assessment. It stands for Symptoms, Allergies, Medications, Past medical history, Last oral intake, and Events leading up to the injury or illness. This information provides a comprehensive view of the patient's condition and can guide your care decisions while waiting for professional help.

In wilderness settings, where professional medical help might be hours or even days away, your assessments need to be thorough but efficient. Time is often against you, and environmental conditions can rapidly worsen a patient's state. Your ability to accurately perform these assessments and take appropriate action can significantly impact the outcome. Even with limited resources, understanding the basics of these assessments empowers you to make informed decisions.

Equipment plays a pivotal role in assessments. From using a simple flashlight for checking pupil responses to understanding how to improvise splints from natural materials, your kit and knowledge transform you into the most valuable resource in a crisis. Regular checks on your first aid kit to ensure it's stocked and familiarizing yourself with each item's use cannot be overstated.

Importantly, the primary and secondary assessments are not one-off checks. They are ongoing processes, especially in dynamic and unpredictable wilderness environments. The victim's condition can change rapidly, necessitating repeat assessments and possibly altering your course of action based on new findings.

Adapting to the situation is a critical skill in wilderness first aid. Not every scenario can be textbook-defined, and often, you'll need to think on your feet. Taking a methodical approach to assessments allows you the flexibility to respond effectively as situations evolve. Trusting your training and instincts is crucial in these moments.

Emotionally, performing these assessments under pressure can be challenging. Cultivating a calm demeanor not only helps you think clearly but can also provide much-needed reassurance to the victim. Your confidence can be a beacon of hope in a crisis, underscoring the importance of mental preparedness alongside physical readiness.

Training and continuous learning cannot be underestimated. Engaging in regular refresher courses, practicing scenarios, and deepening your knowledge through additional resources plays a significant role in your effectiveness as a first responder in the wilderness. The landscape of wilderness medicine is always advancing, and staying updated with the latest guidelines and techniques is crucial.

Lastly, remember that even the most seasoned professionals might encounter scenarios that test their limits. In moments of doubt, focusing on the foundation of 'Do no harm' guides your actions. Always prioritize stabilizing and protecting the victim within your capacity, and never hesitate to seek more experienced help when available.

In conclusion, mastering the art of primary and secondary assessments in wilderness first aid is not just about the technical execution but also about embodying the qualities of leadership, calm under pressure, and adaptability. The wilderness demands respect and preparation, and by honing these skills, you prepare not just to survive but to thrive in the face of emergencies. Let every trip into the great outdoors deepen your commitment to learning and readiness, for in the heart of adventure lies the promise of coming back stronger, wiser, and more connected to the wild and oneself.

Calling for Help in the Wild

In the heart of the wilderness, facing an emergency underscores the vital importance of knowing not just how, but when to call for help. Imagine you're miles from the nearest road, your adventure taking an unexpected turn. It's here, amidst the raw beauty of nature, that your ability to signal for assistance could mean the difference between a story of survival and a tale of caution. The art of calling for help transcends basic knowledge; it embodies the spirit of resilience, resourcefulness, and preparation. It's essential to assess the situation coolly—determining the severity and considering if moving the injured could worsen their condition. If the answer is a resolute yes to calling for help, your next steps should tap into the wisdom of both traditional and modern methods. From the timeless signal fires and ground-to-air symbols recognized worldwide, to the cutting-edge satellite messengers and PLBs (Personal Locator Beacons) that send your SOS with pinpoint accuracy, every choice you make should leverage your surroundings and tools at hand. This wisdom not only offers a beacon of hope in times of dire need but also weaves a deeper connection with the wild, reminding us that even in our most vulnerable moments, we're never completely alone. Through preparation, understanding, and the courage to take decisive action, calling for help in the wild transforms from a daunting task into an empowering testament to human will and interconnectedness.

When and How to Signal for Assistance

The wilderness offers an unparalleled sense of freedom, but with that liberty comes the responsibility of being prepared for emergencies. As you navigate through this chapter, remember that the skills you acquire here are not just for your safety but also for the well-being of those who venture into the wild with you. Recognizing when to signal for assistance and knowing the most effective ways to do so can mean the difference between a manageable situation and a crisis.

First, it's crucial to understand that the need to signal for help can arise from various scenarios – whether it's due to an injury, getting lost, or encountering hazardous weather conditions. The key is not to wait until the situation becomes dire. If you're questioning whether it's time to call for help, it probably is. Early intervention can prevent a predicament from escalating into a life-threatening situation.

Before heading out, always inform someone about your plans, including your destination, route, and expected return time. This pre-trip step is essential because if you fail to return as scheduled, rescuers will have a starting point. This piece of advice may seem simple, but in the urgency to explore, it's often overlooked.

Signaling for help can be executed in various ways, from using technological devices to employing age-old visual and auditory signals. Technology offers some of the most effective methods. Devices such as Personal Locator Beacons (PLBs) and satellite messengers can send distress signals with your location to search and rescue teams, operating effectively even in remote areas where mobile phones fail.

However, don't rely solely on technology. Batteries die, and devices can malfunction or get lost. That's why knowing traditional signaling techniques remains critical. The universal distress signal, consisting of three of anything – be it blasts on a whistle, fires, flashes of light, or even groups of rocks – communicates a need for help. This signal transcends language barriers, making it universally recognized across the globe.

Visual signals include using mirrors or any reflective object to catch the sun's rays and direct them towards a search plane or rescue team. This method can attract attention from miles away. At night, a flashlight or a strobe light serves a similar purpose. Remember, three flashes in succession serve as an international distress signal.

If you're immobilized or prefer not to leave your location, creating a large, visible distress signal on the ground can make you more noticeable from the air. Using logs, rocks, or even creating trenches in the snow to spell out "SOS" or "HELP" can significantly increase your chances of being found. These signals should be made as large as possible to increase visibility from the air.

In terms of auditory signals, a whistle is a lightweight, must-have tool. Three sharp blasts at regular intervals are a recognized call for help. Unlike the human voice, a whistle's sharp pitch can cut through the ambient noise of the wilderness and can be heard over long distances.

Fire can also serve as a potent signal, especially at night or in cold, wet conditions where its warmth and light are unmistakable. If possible, creating three fires in a triangle or in a straight line, which is another internationally recognized distress signal, can grab the attention of rescuers. When creating a signal fire, ensure it's controlled and in a clearing to prevent unintended wildfires and to increase visibility to search teams.

Lastly, don't underestimate the power of color contrast and movement to attract attention. Waving a bright-colored piece of fabric or any available high-contrast material can catch the eye of a passing rescuer. If you're with a group, spacing out and creating a moving line can be an effective way to signal for help, as human movement in the wilderness is an unusual sight and can prompt a quicker response.

While signaling for help, conserve your energy and resources. If you're using a mirror or a flashlight, for instance, use it selectively when you hear or see potential rescuers nearby. This strategy not only preserves battery life but also ensures that your signals are targeted and effective.

Emotionally, it's essential to stay calm and maintain hope. Rescuers are trained to find those who are lost, and by effectively signaling for help, you're greatly improving your chances of being found. Trust in the skills you have and the preparations you've made.

An important part of being able to signal effectively is practicing these techniques before you find yourself in an emergency situation. Whether it's learning to use a signal mirror without blinding yourself or getting the hang of blowing a whistle in bursts of three, familiarity with these techniques will make them second nature when you truly need them.

Finally, remember that signaling for assistance is not a sign of defeat. On the contrary, it's a proactive, strategic decision that prioritizes safety and well-being. It reflects a deep respect for the power and unpredictability of nature. As adventurers, respecting our limits and recognizing when we need help is as important as any survival skill we learn. So, venture forth with confidence, but never underestimate the importance of preparation and the wisdom of seeking help when the situation demands it.

Chapter 4:
Responding to Environmental Hazards

In the realm of wilderness adventures and outdoor escapades, knowledge is more than just power—it's survival. This chapter is a treasure trove of strategies and wisdom for thriving in the face of environmental hazards. From the searing heat waves that appear to melt the horizon to the bone-chilling cold that can freeze the spirit of any explorer, nature's extremes demand respect and readiness. Here, you'll learn not only to recognize the early signs of heat exhaustion and hypothermia but also the immediate, life-saving treatments that can be administered even when far from civilization. But it doesn't stop with temperature-related dangers; higher altitudes bring their own set of challenges. Altitude sickness, a condition too often underestimated, has the potential to turn a mountainous adventure into a perilous ordeal. Armed with preventative measures and acute care techniques, you'll ascend with confidence, knowing you're prepared to face what lies above. This chapter isn't just about survival—it's about empowerment. As you turn these pages, you're gaining the wisdom to not only face the wilderness but to embrace its untamed beauty with a sense of security and resilience.

Heat-Related Illnesses

In the grand theater of the wilderness, where every tree, stone, and river tells a story of resilience, heat-related illnesses stand as formidable adversaries to outdoor enthusiasts and professionals alike. Venturing into the heart of nature requires not just courage but an understanding of how the body reacts to the sweltering embrace of heat. As we peel back the layers of heat-related ailments, it's essential to recognize the signs of dehydration, heat exhaustion, and the more severe, heat stroke. Each condition, if left unchecked, can rapidly escalate, transforming an adventure into a survival scenario. Armed with knowledge and preventive measures, such as adequate hydration, proper clothing, and acclimatization strategies, you're empowered to face the sun's relentless fury. But when the inevitable strikes, and it will, knowing how to cool the body efficiently and seek immediate medical attention could mean the difference between life and a dire outcome. This segment is a call to action—a reminder that amidst the vast beauty of our world, preparation and respect for the environment's power are your true allies. Let's embrace the challenge, ready to adapt, survive, and thrive, for the wilderness teaches us not just to endure but to flourish under the sun's dominion.

Recognition and Treatment

Continuing from the foundation laid in the previous chapters, let's delve into the critical aspects of recognizing various conditions and administering the appropriate treatment in wilderness settings. In these environments, being prepared and knowledgeable can make the difference between a swift recovery and a severe complication. Whether you're facing the scorching heat of a desert trek, the bone-chilling cold of a mountain expedition, or the unexpected bite in a serene forest, understanding how to recognize and treat common ailments is your gateway to not just surviving, but thriving in the wild.

Heat-related illnesses are a significant risk in hot environments, especially during strenuous activities. The early recognition of symptoms such as excessive sweating, weakness, dizziness, and nausea can prevent the escalation to heat stroke, a life-threatening condition characterized by a high body temperature and altered mental state. Immediate treatment involves moving the affected individual to a cooler area, applying cool, wet cloths to the skin, and providing hydration. This proactive response can be lifesaving, emphasizing the power of timely intervention.

Conversely, cold-related injuries pose a stark contrast in symptoms but require an equally strategic approach for treatment. Hypothermia, defined by a drop in the body's core temperature, begins with shivering, fatigue, and confusion. Recognizing these signs early is crucial, as delayed treatment can lead to severe consequences. The initial care involves removing any wet clothing, providing insulation and warmth, and offering warm, non-alcoholic fluids if the victim is conscious. This method underscores the necessity of understanding and combating the environment's impact on the body.

Altitude sickness is another condition that can catch many off guard, characterized by headaches, nausea, and dizziness due to the lower oxygen levels at high elevations. Recognizing these indicators early and responding with rest, hydration, and gradual acclimatization can prevent more severe forms of altitude sickness, showcasing the importance of listening to your body and responding appropriately.

Snake bites, while less common, present a unique challenge requiring specific knowledge for correct treatment. First aid steps include keeping the victim calm, immobilizing the bitten limb, and seeking immediate medical attention. It's a testament to the principle that sometimes, the best treatment is rapid evacuation and expert care.

Insect bites and stings, more frequent than snake bites, usually result in minor symptoms that can be managed with over-the-counter treatments for relief from pain and itching. However, recognizing signs of an allergic reaction, such as difficulty breathing and swelling of the face or throat, is vital for immediate intervention. This scenario highlights the unpredictability of nature and the importance of preparedness for all eventualities.

When it comes to wound care, recognizing the severity of the wound is the first step. Cleaning and dressing wounds properly to prevent infection is paramount, especially in environments where medical help is not readily available. The ability to assess and respond to wounds showcases the critical nature of first aid knowledge in preserving health and preventing complications.

Managing bleeding involves direct pressure, elevation of the injured area, and, when necessary, the use of tourniquets. The decision to use a tourniquet must be informed and decisive, balancing the immediate need to stop life-threatening bleeding against the potential for long-term complications.

Shock, a life-threatening condition resulting from insufficient blood flow, can develop rapidly after an injury or allergic reaction. Recognizing the signs of shock, including rapid pulse, shallow breathing, and cool, clammy skin, allows for prompt intervention. Initial care focuses on maintaining airway, breathing, and circulation, and keeping the victim warm and comfortable until professional help can be reached.

In cases of fractures and sprains, the RICE technique - Rest, Ice, Compression, Elevation - serves as an effective initial response. However, recognizing the difference between a fracture and a sprain is crucial for appropriate care, emphasizing the need for a thorough assessment and cautious management.

Drowning recognition and the immediate response can be the thin line between life and death. Fast recognition of distress and implementing safe rescue and initial care techniques are critical skills for anyone frequenting water bodies. This reality spotlights the imperative of vigilance and readiness in all situations.

Building on these specific treatments, it's evident that knowledge, while powerful, is only as effective as its application. Every response to a given condition, from the heat of the desert to the cold of the high mountains, requires not just a textbook understanding, but a mindset prepared for action, adaptability, and resilience.

This journey through the recognition and treatment of various conditions in the wilderness brings us to a fundamental truth: the wild, with all its beauty and brutality, is not a realm to be feared but respected and understood. It demands from us not just physical strength, but the mental fortitude to learn, prepare, and adapt. And in this demand lies an invitation to become not just survivors, but guardians of our own lives and the lives of those around us.

With each step into the unknown, let us carry not just our gear, but the weight of responsibility and the light of knowledge. For in the heart of the wilderness lies not just the challenge of survival, but the promise of discovery. It beckons us not to conquer, but to harmonize – to learn its secrets, respect its might, and thrive within its embrace.

In conclusion, recognition and treatment in the wilderness are about more than procedures and protocols; they are about embodying the spirit of preparedness, resilience, and respect for nature. As you venture into the great outdoors, armed with the knowledge from this book, remember that the greatest tool at your disposal is your ability to adapt, learn, and above all, believe in your capacity to overcome. The wilderness awaits, not as a foc but as a teacher. May your journeys be safe, enlightening, and filled with the joy of discovery.

Cold-Related Injuries

The wilderness doesn't yield its beauty without a fair share of challenges, and among these, cold-related injuries stand out as a prime concern for outdoor enthusiasts and professionals alike. Venturing into the cold without acknowledging the risk of hypothermia and frostbite is akin to walking blindfolded into a maze. Hypothermia, an insidious enemy, creeps up when your body loses heat faster than it can produce, clouding judgment and weakening resolve. Frostbite, its cruel companion, targets the extremities, freezing flesh and spirit alike. But fear not, for knowledge is your beacon and preparation your shield. Understanding the signs, such as uncontrollable shivering, numbness, and fatigue, can turn the tide before it's too late. Immediate intervention, including finding shelter, rewarming, and hydration, transforms potential tragedy into tales of triumph. Let this resonate within you: survival in the cold is not solely about battling the elements, but embracing the wisdom to respect and respond to them. As you equip yourself with the right tools and techniques, let the spirit of resilience guide you through the frost, for it is in challenging the wilderness that we truly discover our strength.

Hypothermia and Frostbite Management

Venturing into the wilderness, whether for leisure, adventure, or professional necessity, carries implicit challenges, among which are the harsh realities of cold-related injuries. Every outdoor enthusiast must equip themselves with the knowledge to combat two formidable adversaries: hypothermia and frostbite. Understanding these conditions, recognizing their signs, and knowing the steps to manage them can be the difference between life and harrowing consequences.

At its core, hypothermia occurs when the body loses heat faster than it can produce it, leading to a dangerously low body temperature. This condition can creep upon an individual insidiously, making its recognition crucial. The initial signs may include shivering, which is the body's natural response to generate heat, but as hypothermia progresses, coordination falters, confusion sets in, and energy wanes, making even simple tasks seem Herculean.

To manage hypothermia, the first step is to prevent further heat loss. Moving the affected individual to shelter can make a significant difference. Replacing wet clothing with dry, insulating layers helps trap body heat. Use of blankets, sleeping bags, or even body-to-body contact can aid in rewarming. Warm, sweet beverages can provide internal warmth, but avoid alcohol or caffeine, which can exacerbate the problem.

Frostbite represents the injury to body tissues caused by freezing, typically affecting extremities like fingers, toes, ears, and the nose. The danger lies not only in the frostbite itself but in its potential to cause permanent damage or loss of the affected areas. Recognizing frostbite involves noting the hard, pale, and cold qualities of the affected tissues, often followed by numbness or aching.

The key to managing frostbite is gentle rewarming. Direct heat can damage the tissue further, so immersion in warm (not hot) water is preferred. It's essential to avoid rubbing or applying pressure to the frozen areas, as the tissue can be very fragile. After rewarming, the area should be dried and wrapped to keep it warm and protected.

One cannot overstate the importance of prevention when it comes to hypothermia and frostbite. Proper preparation entails not only bringing adequate gear but also understanding how to use it effectively. Layering clothing allows for the adjustment of insulation as activity levels and weather conditions change, a crucial strategy in maintaining core body temperature.

Hydration and nutrition also play critical roles in cold-weather safety. A well-nourished and hydrated body generates heat more efficiently, so regular intake of food and warm, non-caffeinated beverages can provide an internal source of warmth.

Should an individual fall victim to hypothermia or frostbite, quick action can prevent the situation from worsening. It's imperative to recognize that these conditions are medical emergencies. If symptoms of either condition are observed, seek professional medical assistance immediately. While awaiting help, employ the management strategies mentioned to promote rewarming and protect the individual from further exposure.

Building an emergency shelter can provide temporary protection from the cold, wind, and precipitation. Knowing how to construct a basic shelter using natural materials or a survival kit can make a significant difference in severe conditions.

As efforts are made to stabilize an individual affected by cold injuries, maintaining morale becomes an important aspect. The power of positive thinking and encouragement can bolster the spirits of the affected person and the group, contributing to a more effective response to the emergency.

Let's also emphasize the significance of learning and practicing first aid skills before venturing into the wilderness. Courses offered by reputable organizations provide invaluable hands-on experience, preparing adventurers to respond confidently to emergencies, including hypothermia and frostbite.

Interestingly, technologies and innovations in outdoor gear continue to evolve, offering better protection against the cold. Investing in high-quality, weather-appropriate equipment can enhance safety and comfort, reducing the risk of cold-related injuries.

Cold weather adventures offer a unique charm and challenge, inviting the prepared and the prudent. Understanding the risks, including hypothermia and frostbite, and knowing how to manage them, empowers outdoor enthusiasts to safely enjoy the magic of the winter wilderness. It's this preparation, awareness, and resilience that turn potential disasters into tales of triumph and survival.

In conclusion, while the wilderness beckons with its beauty and mysteries, it does not forgive ignorance or unpreparedness. Hypothermia and frostbite are but two of the risks that await the unready. Yet, with knowledge, preparation, and respect for nature's power, adventurers can face these challenges head-on. They can navigate through the cold, emerge stronger, and with stories that inspire courage and a deep reverence for the wild. Let this understanding guide your preparations and ensure that your adventures bring joy and awe, rather than peril.

Altitude Sickness

Ascending to high elevations brings the adventure of towering peaks and breathtaking views, but it can also introduce the risk of altitude sickness, a condition that demands respect and understanding. Altitude sickness occurs when your body can't get enough oxygen from the air at high altitudes, leading to symptoms such as headache, nausea, and dizziness. The key to prevention lies in a gradual ascent, allowing your body the time it needs to adjust to the thinner air. Should symptoms arise, it's critical to recognize them early and take immediate action, which may include descending to a lower altitude or using medications prescribed for altitude sickness. Remember, your safety and health are paramount. With the right knowledge and preparation, you can minimize the risks and ensure your high-altitude adventures are memorable for all the right reasons. Embrace the challenge, but do so with caution and respect for the power of nature and the limits of your own body.

Prevention and Care

As we venture into the wild, embracing the raw and untamed beauty of nature, ensuring our safety becomes paramount. Adventure calls to our spirit, urging us to explore, but it also demands our respect and caution. The wilderness, while breathtaking, is unforgiving, and a single misstep can lead to serious consequences. Thus, the cornerstone of wilderness first aid isn't just about responding to injuries—it's about preventing them. This chapter is dedicated to equipping you with the knowledge and strategies to avoid common outdoor hazards and care for issues should they arise.

Preventative measures are the shields against the potential dangers that lurk in the great outdoors. Before stepping out into the wilderness, it's essential to familiarize yourself with the environment you'll be entering. Understanding the geography, weather patterns, and potential wildlife encounters can dramatically reduce your risk of injury or illness. Pre-trip planning and preparation lay the groundwork for safety, allowing you to anticipate challenges and equip yourself accordingly.

Hydration and nutrition can't be overlooked. The wilderness can quickly sap your strength, turning a journey into a perilous ordeal. Adequate hydration maintains your physical and mental capabilities, preventing the dangerous onset of conditions like heat stroke or hypothermia. Similarly, proper nutrition fuels your body for the demands of the trail. Simple precautions, like bringing water purification methods and high-energy foods, can significantly impact your well-being in the wild.

One of the most effective ways to prevent injury is to ensure that you have the appropriate gear. From protective clothing to safeguard against the elements to durable footwear that provides stability and traction, what you wear can be your first line of defense. Don't underestimate the importance of quality gear—it can offer protection from severe weather, prevent falls, and even deter wildlife encounters.

Training cannot be understated. Whether it's a formal wilderness first aid course or practicing navigation skills, education empowers you. Knowing how to react in an emergency, whether it's administering CPR, managing an unexpected wildlife encounter, or signaling for help, can make the difference between life and death. Regularly refresh your skills to ensure you're ready to face the challenges that nature might throw your way.

Communication plans are vital. Always inform someone about your itinerary and expected return time. In many wilderness areas, cell service is non-existent. Consider carrying a satellite phone, personal locator beacon, or other emergency signaling devices. These tools can be lifesavers, enabling rescue services to locate you swiftly in case of an emergency.

When it comes to caring for injuries or illnesses in the wilderness, prompt and correct action can prevent a situation from worsening. The key to effective care is calm and decisive action. Assess the situation thoroughly before jumping into action, ensuring you're not putting yourself or the injured party in further danger.

For minor injuries like cuts and scrapes, cleaning the wound promptly and applying a sterile dressing can prevent infection. In case of more serious injuries, such as fractures or large wounds, stabilizing the injury and preventing further damage is crucial until professional medical help can be reached. Techniques such as splinting a broken limb can be vital skills to know.

Recognizing symptoms of common wilderness-related illnesses and conditions, such as hypothermia, heat exhaustion, altitude sickness, or dehydration, is equally important. Early recognition followed by immediate and appropriate care can prevent the condition from escalating into a life-threatening situation. For example, moving someone out of direct sunlight and providing them with fluids can be a simple yet effective way to manage heat exhaustion.

Allergic reactions in the wilderness, particularly those from insect bites or plants, can quickly become emergencies. Carrying antihistamines and knowing how to use an EpiPen can save a life in these situations. It's crucial to understand and recognize the signs of severe allergic reactions to act quickly.

When it comes to wildlife, the best strategy is prevention through awareness and respect. Educate yourself about the wildlife you might encounter, maintain a safe distance, and store food properly to avoid attracting animals to your campsite. If an encounter does occur, having knowledge about how to react can prevent the situation from escalating.

Environmental hazards such as rivers, cliffs, and steep terrain require caution and respect. Assess the risks before attempting to navigate these obstacles. When in doubt, turning back is always a better option than pushing forward and risking injury.

Fire safety is another crucial aspect of wilderness prevention and care. Forest fires can be devastating and are often accidentally started by unattended or poorly managed campfires. Understanding how to safely start, maintain, and extinguish a campfire is a responsibility every wilderness adventurer should take seriously.

Lastly, mental preparedness plays a critical role in both the prevention of emergencies and the care of injuries. Panic and fear can cloud judgment, leading to poor decision-making. Techniques that enhance mental resilience and promote calm can be invaluable in a crisis. Regularly practicing stress-reduction techniques, such as deep breathing or visualization, can help maintain clarity and focus when it matters most.

In conclusion, the art of wilderness survival is as much about prevention as it is about treatment. It's about being prepared, staying informed, and respecting the forces of nature. By adopting a proactive approach to safety, you can enjoy the profound beauty and transformational experiences the wild offers, secure in the knowledge that you're prepared to face whatever comes your way. Remember, nature doesn't bend to our will, but by understanding and respecting its laws, we learn not just to survive, but to thrive.

Chapter 5:
Handling Bites and Stings

In the heart of the wild, the beauty of nature intertwines with its perils, and among these, bites and stings from wildlife present a critical challenge for outdoor enthusiasts. Venturing into the wilderness equips us with not just the thrill of adventure but also the responsibility to prepare for the unexpected. In this chapter, we're diving into the essential knowledge and skills needed to handle snake bites, insect bites and stings, and the frightening yet rare encounters with hostile animals. The wilderness calls to us, inviting us with its untamed mystery, but it's upon us to tread its paths with caution and respect. Drawing from the well of wisdom that our collective experiences offer, we'll explore first aid steps that can be the difference between a minor inconvenience and a life-threatening emergency. With a focus on practical, immediate response tactics, we aim to empower you with the confidence to manage these challenges effectively.

Understanding the nature of the threat, whether it's the alarming surprise of a snake bite, the discomfort of insect bites and stings, or the adrenaline-fueled urgency of an animal attack, is paramount. But it's the calm, collected application of first aid principles that truly makes a difference. From the dos and don'ts for snake bites to the preventative measures against insect nuisances and the decisive actions required to mitigate an animal attack, this chapter serves as a guide to not just survive but to thrive in the face of adversity. Let the knowledge contained in these pages be a beacon of safety, guiding you through the majestic wilderness with confidence and care.

Snake Bites

In the untamed expanses of nature, encountering a snake can't always be avoided, making the knowledge of handling snake bites an indispensable part of wilderness first aid. Upon encountering a snake bite, the initial moments are critical. Begin by remaining calm; excessive movement or panic can accelerate the venom's spread. Ensure the victim's safety by moving them away from the snake to prevent further bites. It's vital to remember not to suck out the venom, cut the wound, or apply ice or tourniquets, as these methods do more harm than good. Instead, keep the affected limb immobilized and at heart level to manage the venom's spread without quickening it. The importance of seeking professional medical help cannot be overstressed — time is of the essence. While awaiting help, covering the bite with a clean, dry dressing is a proactive step. In these moments, your actions are powered by knowledge, determination, and a poised demeanor, embodying the cardinal tenets of wilderness survival. This knowledge doesn't just prepare you for the unpredictable; it transforms you into a beacon of hope and resilience, empowering you to stand undaunted in the face of nature's challenges.

First Aid Steps

Embarking on an outdoor adventure in the wild can be both exhilarating and unpredictable. While the beauty and solitude of nature provide a perfect backdrop for adventure, it's crucial to be prepared for any emergencies that may arise. Understanding first aid steps is not just about memorizing procedures; it's about developing a mindset geared towards safety, preparedness, and the willingness to act when faced with adversity.

The first and most critical step in any emergency is to stay calm. Panic can cloud judgment and delay response times, so take a deep breath and focus on the task at hand. Remember, your ability to remain composed can make a significant difference in the outcome of any situation.

Once you've managed to stay calm, it's time to assess the situation. Look around and evaluate the safety of your immediate environment. Is there ongoing danger such as wildfire, rising water, or unstable terrain? Ensuring your safety and that of the injured person is paramount before administering first aid.

After ensuring the area is safe, assess the condition of the person in need. If they are conscious, talk to them. Ask them what happened and where they feel pain. Communication can offer vital clues to what the issue may be. If they are unconscious, check for responsiveness by gently tapping them and shouting. Do not move the person unless necessary, as this may exacerbate their injuries.

If the person is not breathing, start CPR immediately. Chest compressions and rescue breaths could be life-saving. It's a technique that everyone venturing into the wilderness should be familiar with, even though we all hope never to use it. On your adventures, carrying a reliable guidebook for reference can reinforce your memory and confidence in performing CPR.

For bleeding control, applying direct pressure to the wound is critical. Use a clean cloth or bandage and press firmly to stop or slow the bleeding. If the bleeding is severe and does not stop with direct pressure, a tourniquet might be necessary, but this should be used as a last resort and only if you are trained on how to do so properly.

In cases of fractures or sprains, immobilizing the injured limb or joint can reduce pain and prevent further injury. Use splints made from available materials if necessary, but ensure they do not restrict circulation. Remember, the goal is to provide support and stabilization, not to cut off blood flow.

For burns, immediately move the person away from the source of the burn, if safe to do so. Cool the burn with clean, cool water, but do not apply ice, which can cause further tissue damage. Cover the burn with a sterile, non-adhesive bandage or cloth to protect the area from infection.

When dealing with environmental illnesses such as hypothermia or heat stroke, it's essential to act swiftly. For hypothermia, gently warm the person with blankets and shared body heat, avoiding direct heat sources. For heat stroke, move the person to a cooler place, apply cool, wet cloths to their skin, and provide sips of water if they're conscious.

Encountering wildlife bites or stings requires specific care. For snake bites, keep the bitten limb immobilized and below heart level if possible, and seek medical help immediately. Avoid suction, cutting around the wound, or using a tourniquet. For insect stings, remove the stinger if present, wash the area, and apply a cold pack to reduce swelling.

Dehydration is a common issue in wilderness settings. Encourage the person to drink water slowly if they are conscious and able to swallow. Avoid giving them food or drinks that can dehydrate them further, such as caffeine or alcohol.

Recognizing the signs of shock, which can include rapid pulse, shallow breathing, and cold, clammy skin, is crucial. Keep the person warm and comfortable, elevate their legs if there are no injuries suggesting otherwise, and seek emergency medical help as soon as possible.

In the event of an allergic reaction, if the person has an epinephrine injector (EpiPen), assist them in using it, or administer it yourself if they are unable. Monitor their breathing and swallow ability closely and prepare to perform CPR if necessary.

Finally, the importance of practice cannot be overstated. Regularly refreshing your knowledge and skills through courses, workshops, and revisiting instructional materials will ensure you're prepared for a variety of first aid scenarios. Being equipped with the right knowledge and skills can make you a valuable asset to any outdoor adventure and potentially save lives.

Remember, the wilderness demands respect, and part of that respect is being prepared. Whether you're a seasoned adventurer or a weekend warrior, taking the time to learn and understand first aid steps is an investment in safety that can pay dividends in the most critical moments. Carry these lessons with you, and let them empower your adventures, ensuring that you and those around you can safely enjoy the beauty and majesty of the great outdoors.

Insect Bites and Stings

When venturing into the vast expanse of the wilderness, our interactions with nature can sometimes leave us with souvenirs in the form of insect bites and stings. However, these minor setbacks shouldn't deter the spirit of adventure. Armed with the right knowledge and tools, anyone can transform these challenges into mere blips on the exhilarating journey of outdoor exploration. Recognizing the signs of more serious reactions is vital; symptoms such as difficulty breathing, swelling of the face or lips, or hives, suggest an allergic reaction requiring immediate attention. For most bites and stings, treatment involves removing the stinger if present, cleaning the area with soap and water, applying ice to reduce swelling, and considering antihistamines to alleviate itching. Preventive measures can't be overstated—wearing protective clothing, using insect repellent, and avoiding known habitats of aggressive insects are simple yet effective strategies. Remember, knowledge is as crucial to wilderness exploration as a compass. Every mark left by nature is a reminder of our resilience, and with every step forward, we become more adept at navigating the challenges, turning obstacles into opportunities for growth and learning.

Treatment and Prevention

Within the expanse of the wilderness, every adventurer's primary goal is to enjoy the beauty and challenges it presents. However, this comes with the responsibility of being prepared for potential hazards. In this section, we delve into practical steps to treat injuries and illnesses, while emphasizing the paramount importance of prevention. Understanding and applying these principles can be the difference between a minor hicoper and a life-threatening situation.

The key to managing injuries and illnesses in the wilderness begins with a sound prevention strategy. This includes educating yourself on potential hazards specific to the area you're exploring, whether they be environmental, such as extreme temperatures, or biological, like venomous creatures. Preparation, which encompasses both physical readiness and a properly equipped first aid kit, cannot be overstated. It's essential to tailor your first aid kit to your adventure, ensuring you have the necessary supplies to address the common risks associated with your specific outdoor activity.

When it comes to treating injuries, remember that your primary goal is to stabilize the individual until professional medical help can be reached. This may mean performing first aid techniques such as applying pressure to stop bleeding, splinting a broken limb, or administering CPR. Each of these actions can significantly impact the outcome for the injured party, potentially saving a life.

For bites and stings, rapid assessment and appropriate action are crucial. If you're dealing with a snake bite, for example, keeping the victim calm and immobilized can slow the spread of venom. Meanwhile, treat insect bites and stings by removing the stinger if present, washing the area, and applying a cold pack to reduce swelling.

In cases of environmental hazards like heatstroke or hypothermia, understanding the signs and initiating immediate treatment can prevent the situation from worsening. For heatstroke, move the individual to a cooler location, apply cool, wet cloths or ice to their body, and provide sips of water if they're conscious. With hypothermia, warming the person gradually is key; remove any wet clothing and use dry blankets or your own body heat to warm them.

Altitude sickness is another concern that shouldn't be underestimated. If symptoms occur, the best treatment is descent. Prevention strategies include acclimatization over several days, staying hydrated, and avoiding overexertion.

Water safety is also paramount. Always wear a life jacket when in or around water, regardless of your swimming proficiency. Learn and practice self-rescue techniques as well as safe ways to assist others without putting yourself in danger. Recognizing the signs of drowning and understanding how to perform safe rescue and resuscitation can make all the difference.

Wound care in the wilderness requires diligence to prevent infection. Clean wounds thoroughly with clean water, and dress them with sterile bandages. Regularly inspect wounds for signs of infection. If you're traveling in areas where water quality is a concern, carrying a water purification method is a must to ensure you have access to clean water for wound care and hydration.

One of the most critical aspects of wilderness first aid is the ability to manage bleeding. Knowing how to apply direct pressure, use a tourniquet when necessary, and protect the wound from contaminants are skills that can prevent a manageable situation from becoming dire.

Shock management is another area where knowledge and calm action can significantly impact survival. Keep the person warm, calm, and horizontal with elevated legs, if possible, to promote circulation while waiting for evacuation or emergency responders.

For fractures and sprains, remember the RICE method (Rest, Ice, Compression, Elevation). Splinting the affected area can prevent further injury. However, ensure you're trained in how to properly apply a splint to avoid causing more harm.

Prevention of chronic conditions flare-ups, such as asthma or diabetes, relies on thorough pre-trip planning. Ensure you have an adequate supply of medications, understand how your condition might interact with the challenges of the wilderness, and have a plan in place for monitoring and managing your condition.

Finally, never underestimate the power of mental preparedness. The wilderness can be as taxing mentally as it is physically. Techniques for managing panic and anxiety, alongside the physical first aid skills, can ensure that you and your companions remain calm and capable in the face of unexpected challenges.

In conclusion, the key to effective treatment and prevention in wilderness first aid lies in education, preparation, and the calm execution of learned first aid techniques. By equipping yourself with knowledge and skills, you embrace the power to make your adventures safer and more enjoyable. More than just surviving in the wild, it's about thriving and ensuring the well-being of yourself and those around you, no matter what nature has in store.

Remember, the wilderness invites us to step into a world beyond our own, to test our limits and explore the beauty of the natural world. Equipped with the right knowledge and skills, you're not just a visitor;

you're a guardian of your own safety and an advocate for the preservation of these precious environments. Let's carry the torch of preparedness and respect, lighting the way for countless safe and enriching adventures to come.

Animal Attacks

In the untamed wilderness, encounters with wildlife can swiftly escalate from awe-inspiring to life-threatening. The key to surviving animal attacks lies not just in how you react but in the proactive steps you take to avoid such confrontations. Should you find yourself face-to-face with a wild animal, your immediate response should be guided by a clear understanding of the species you're dealing with and the situation at hand. This section delves into essential tactics for handling encounters with potentially dangerous animals, distinguishing between defensive actions to deter an attack and the vital steps to take if an attack cannot be avoided. Whether it's maintaining a calm demeanor, using noise to deter an animal, or employing a defensive posture to make yourself less of a target, knowing what to do can make all the difference. Moreover, we'll navigate through the aftermath of an attack, focusing on self-assessment for injuries, the importance of seeking medical attention no matter the perceived severity, and the psychological impact such encounters can have. Arm yourself with knowledge, for it's your most powerful weapon against the unpredictability of nature.

Immediate Response Tactics

When confronted with an animal attack in the wilderness, the key to survival and minimizing injury lies in your immediate response. Handling such encounters requires calmness, preparedness, and a knowledge of the specific behaviors of potential animal threats you might face. Whether it's a bear, a mountain lion, or a less intimidating, yet still dangerous, animal like a raccoon or fox, each situation demands a set of responses tailored to ensure your safety and that of those with you.

The initial moments following an animal attack are critical. First and foremost, it's imperative to assess the situation quickly. Look around to understand the context of the attack. Is the animal feeling threatened? Are you near its young? Understanding the motive can guide your immediate actions. If it's possible and safe, slowly back away from the animal, maintaining a calm demeanor and avoiding sudden movements that could further provoke the animal.

In the event of a bear attack, the specific species of bear can dictate your response. For grizzly encounters, playing dead can sometimes deter the bear from continuing its attack. Lay flat on your stomach, cover the back of your neck with your hands, and spread your legs slightly apart to make it harder for the bear to turn you over. Conversely, if you're dealing with a black bear, fighting back with anything you have might be your best chance of survival.

Mountain lion attacks require a different approach. If faced with a mountain lion, make yourself appear as large and menacing as possible. Hold your ground, make noise, and try to look more intimidating. Fight back vigorously if attacked, targeting the animal's face and eyes.

In the case of snake bites, identifying the type of snake can be beneficial, but it's not vital for initial treatment. The priority is to keep the bitten limb immobilized and at heart level, and seek medical help immediately. Do not attempt to suck out the venom or apply tourniquets. These methods are not only ineffective but can also worsen the situation.

When dealing with insect bites and stings, removing the stinger without squeezing it is crucial to prevent additional venom from entering the wound. Wash the area with soap and water, apply a cold pack to reduce swelling, and monitor for signs of an allergic reaction such as difficulty breathing or a rapid heartbeat.

For larger animal attacks resulting in severe wounds, immediate wound care is essential. Controlling bleeding by applying direct pressure with a clean cloth or bandage is a priority. If the injury is life-threatening and medical help is not immediately available, a tourniquet may become necessary. Remember, a tourniquet should be used only as a last resort.

Regardless of the animal encounter, shock is a genuine concern. Symptoms include cold and clammy skin, rapid pulse, rapid breathing, nausea, or vomiting. Laying the person down with their legs elevated can help manage shock until medical assistance can be reached. Cover them with a blanket to maintain body heat.

Communication with your group during and after an animal attack is vital. If you're hiking or camping in a group, have pre-determined signals for help or danger. After an incident, regroup at a safe location, count off to ensure everyone is present, and discuss if a change in plans is necessary.

After ensuring everyone's immediate safety and tending to any injuries, debrief with your group about the attack. Discussing what happened, even briefly, can provide critical information for avoiding future attacks and can also be a cathartic experience for those involved.

Preparation before heading into wilderness areas can't be overstressed. Educate yourself and your group on the wildlife native to the area you'll be exploring. Knowledge about animal behavior can significantly affect the outcome of a wildlife encounter.

Carrying an emergency whistle and bear spray (where permitted) can provide a means of deterrence in unexpected animal encounters. Knowing how to use these tools effectively before you need them can make a difference in critical moments.

If an animal encounter results in an injury, after-care is just as important as the immediate response. Monitoring for signs of infection, ensuring tetanus vaccination are up-to-date, and seeking professional medical evaluation as soon as possible can prevent complications down the line.

Beyond the physical implications, the mental impact of an animal attack can be profound. Acknowledge the trauma and consider seeking professional support to cope with any psychological after-effects. Nature can be unpredictable, and it's crucial to address the emotional toll such encounters can take.

In conclusion, while the wilderness offers beauty, solitude, and adventure, it's not without its risks. A respectful awareness of our place in nature, combined with a knowledge of immediate response tactics, can ensure that our adventures in the great outdoors remain safe and fulfilling. Remember, preparation doesn't detract from the adventure; it enhances it by ensuring we can confidently face any challenge the wild throws our way.

Chapter 6:
Wound Care in the Wilderness

In the heart of the wilderness, where nature's beauty meets unpredictability, the mastery of wound care becomes an invaluable skill in your adventure's toolkit. Venturing beyond the beaten path is not without its hazards, and a wound, if improperly managed, can escalate from a minor nuisance to a critical emergency. The essence of wound care in the great outdoors is not just about cleaning and dressing wounds; it's about understanding the environment's challenges and responding with precision and confidence.

Embracing the wilderness with its inherent risks requires a mindset that blends resilience with knowledge. When it comes to wound management, your first line of defense is always prevention. However, when you're confronted with a wound, knowing how to effectively clean and dress it can make all the difference. This chapter will guide you through the techniques and tips essential for dealing with cuts, abrasions, and lacerations. You'll learn how to staunch bleeding with direct pressure, and when necessary, the proper application of a tourniquet. Recognizing the signs of shock and initiating initial care will also be covered, as it's often a critical component of wound management.

Wound care in the wilderness extends beyond the physical aspects; it's about fostering a spirit of self-reliance and calm in the face of adversity. Each technique shared in this chapter is a stepping stone towards becoming more adept in handling emergencies, ultimately empowering you to tackle challenges with a steadfast heart. Whether you're a seasoned adventurer or a weekend warrior, the skills and insights garnered here will equip you to face the unpredictable nature of the wild with confidence and grace.

Cleaning and Dressing Wounds

In the heart of the wilderness, where medical help might be miles away, knowing how to properly clean and dress wounds becomes a cornerstone of first aid that can't be overlooked. This task, seemingly simple, is your first line of defense against infection and the starting point for healing. First, gently clean the wound with clean water to remove any debris or dirt. If clean water isn't available, snow that's been melted and boiled can be a lifesaver. Avoid using river or stream water directly, as it may contain bacteria that could worsen the situation. Once the wound is clean, pat it dry with a clean cloth or bandana. The next step involves dressing the wound to keep it protected. When applying a dressing, ensure it's snug but not too tight, to promote healing and prevent restriction of blood flow. Remember, in the wilderness, resources may be limited, but your ingenuity isn't. Items such as clean pieces of clothing or bandanas can be transformed into effective dressings or bandages. Throughout this process, keep a positive mindset. Your ability to calmly and effectively manage such situations not only ensures physical healing but also instills a sense of confidence and resilience that extends beyond first aid, into every aspect of wilderness adventure.

Techniques and Tips

Techniques and Tips for effective wound care in the wilderness are both an art and a science, melding intuition with practice and knowledge. Wound care isn't just about slapping on a bandage; it's about understanding the wound, the environment, and the resources at hand to foster optimal healing.

Firstly, it's crucial to assess the wound carefully. This means looking beyond the obvious. Is there debris or foreign material embedded? What's the wound's depth? Understanding these factors is the first step toward effective treatment. In the wilderness, your assessment tools are your senses and your experience. Feel around (with gloves on, where possible) for unseen objects and use clean water to gently rinse the wound, observing how it reacts.

Water is your ally but use it wisely. In environments where clean water is limited, prioritize. You may need to use a filter system or boil water before it's deemed safe for wound cleaning. Remember, infection prevention is paramount, and clean water is a key player in this process.

Dressing a wound is more than covering it up. It's about creating an environment conducive to healing. In the wilderness, your first aid kit needs to be versatile. Items like gauze, medical tape, and bandages are standard, but don't overlook natural resources. In some cases, clean, smooth leaves or bark can serve as temporary dressings in a pinch.

The art of improvisation is a must-have skill. For instance, you can use a clean cloth or article of clothing as a bandage if you're out of medical supplies. Similarly, ice from a cold stream, wrapped in fabric, can serve as a makeshift cold compress to reduce swelling around a wound.

Monitoring for infection is an ongoing process. Signs like increased redness, warmth, swelling, or pus are red flags. In the wild, where professional medical help may be days away, early recognition and action can make a significant difference. Keep the wound clean, change dressings regularly, and if you have them, apply antibiotic ointment sparingly.

Understanding when a wound is beyond your capability to manage is a skill in itself. Deep wounds, those with suspected tendon or nerve damage, or those showing signs of infection may require evacuation and professional medical care. This judgment call is crucial and should be based on thorough assessment and the resources at your disposal.

Encourage rest and hydration. The human body heals faster and more effectively when it's well-rested and hydrated. Even if the injury seems minor, encouraging the injured party to take it easy and drink plenty of water can aid significantly in their recovery process.

Splint any injuries near the wound if necessary. A wound on a limb with a fracture or sprain requires immobilization to prevent further injury. Using items from your surroundings, like sticks for splints or clothing for ties, can make a substantial difference in recovery outcomes.

Know when to seek help. Sometimes, the best action is rapid evacuation to a medical facility. Recognizing this need and acting swiftly can be life-saving. Adventure often takes us far from immediate medical care, so activating emergency plans promptly when a wound is severe is a mark of a responsible and knowledgeable caregiver.

Record keeping might seem mundane but jotting down when an injury occurred, when and how you treated it, and any changes in its condition can be incredibly valuable. This information is gold for medical professionals who eventually take over care and can influence treatment decisions.

Elevate whenever possible. Elevation reduces swelling and can slow bleeding in some cases. Use whatever you have to gently elevate the injured area above the heart's level.

Stay informed and practice. Read up on trends in wilderness first aid and practice scenarios before heading out. Knowing what to do and having done it in a calm, controlled environment makes it much easier to recall and perform under stress. This preparation makes you not just a participant in the wilderness but a guardian of it and those you adventure with.

Finally, inspire others with your knowledge and skills. Sharing what you know, teaching others how to treat wounds in the wilderness, and leading by example can have a ripple effect. Your dedication to preparedness and care can empower your fellow adventurers to become more self-reliant and responsible.

In conclusion, wound care in the wilderness demands a balanced approach between using what's available, relying on your knowledge, and knowing when to seek help. It tests your problem-solving abilities, your resolve, and your compassion. Yet, with each challenge faced and overcome, your confidence in navigating these complex situations will grow. The wilderness teaches us that with preparation, perseverance, and positivity, we are capable of facing and overcoming even the most daunting challenges.

Managing Bleeding

In your journey to master wilderness first aid, understanding how to manage bleeding stands as a cornerstone of emergency care. The golden rule? Remain as calm as the undisturbed waters of a mountain lake. When faced with a bleeding wound, your first steps should be direct pressure and, if necessary, the application of a tourniquet. These are your initial allies in the battle to control blood loss. Applying direct pressure with a clean cloth or bandage directly onto the wound helps to stem the flow of blood, allowing the body's natural clotting processes to kick into gear. If direct pressure isn't enough and you're dealing with a life-threatening bleed from an extremity, a tourniquet may become your tool of necessity. Position it between the wound and the heart, tightening until the bleeding stops. Remember, while the use of a tourniquet is a critical life-saving measure, it's a decision made with the gravity of understanding its implications. Each moment in managing wilderness injuries is a step taken on a path leading towards preservation of life and limb, empowering you to stand firm in the face of adversity.

Direct Pressure and Tourniquets

In the wilderness, where help can be hours or even days away, knowing how to manage bleeding is crucial. Life can hinge on these first aid skills and your ability to execute them with confidence and precision. Bleeding, if not controlled, can lead to shock or even be fatal. Here, we dive deep into the methods of direct pressure and tourniquets, essential techniques for managing severe bleeding in the wild.

When confronting a bleeding wound, the first and most effective step is to apply direct pressure. This straightforward method often controls bleeding and allows you to assess the situation more clearly. Use a clean cloth or gauze pad and press firmly over the wound. The goal is to apply enough pressure to stop the flow of blood, but not so much that you cause further injury. This might seem simple, yet it's a powerful tool in your first aid arsenal.

Patience is key. Don't frequently check the wound to see if it has stopped bleeding. Repeatedly removing the pressure to check the wound can disrupt the clotting process. Instead, hold the pressure steadily for at least 10 to 15 minutes before checking. If the bleeding hasn't stopped, apply pressure again, adding more layers if necessary, but never removing the original dressing.

In cases where direct pressure doesn't stop the bleeding, a tourniquet may be your next line of defense. Tourniquets have evolved from battlefield remedies to essential tools in civilian first aid, credited with saving countless lives. A tourniquet is used when bleeding is severe and not controlled by direct pressure, especially if the wound is on an arm or leg.

To use a tourniquet, place it a few inches above the bleeding site, but not over a joint. Tighten it until the bleeding stops. Tourniquets can be improvised from a wide variety of materials, but commercially made tourniquets are more reliable and easier to apply with one hand. It's vital to remember the time of application; write it directly on the tourniquet or on the patient if possible.

There's a myth that applying a tourniquet means sacrificing the limb. This is not accurate. Modern medicine allows for limbs to be saved even after a tourniquet has been applied for several hours. The key is to apply it correctly and ensure that professional medical care is sought immediately.

An important aspect of using a tourniquet is mental readiness. The decision to employ a tourniquet must be swift and decisive. Hesitation can be the difference between a life lost and a life saved. Empower yourself with knowledge and the confidence to act when needed.

Documenting the time a tourniquet was applied is more than a procedural step; it's critical information for medical professionals who will later treat the patient. This simple act of notation can have profound implications on the course of treatment and recovery.

What if you don't have a commercial tourniquet? Improvisation becomes your best friend in the wilderness. Items such as belts, strips of cloth, or bandanas can be used, but ensure that the improvised tourniquet is at least 1 inch wide to avoid damaging the tissue. The key is to apply enough pressure to stop the bleeding without causing additional harm.

After a tourniquet is applied, it is crucial to keep the injured limb immobilized. Any movement can disrupt the clotting process or cause the tourniquet to loosen, leading to more bleeding. Use whatever materials you have to immobilize the limb safely until professional help can be reached.

While managing a bleeding emergency, never forget to protect yourself. Always use gloves if available to reduce the risk of transmitting infections. Your safety is as important as the patient's. It's a delicate balance between offering help and maintaining your well-being.

Communication plays an essential role in emergencies. If you're not alone, delegate tasks to those around you. Someone should be in charge of calling for help while others assist with first aid. Clear communication can streamline the response process and prevent panic.

After applying a tourniquet, monitoring the patient is crucial. Watch for signs of shock and prepare to administer additional first aid if necessary. The wilderness demands respect, and part of that respect includes being prepared for the worst while hoping for the best.

Finally, education is the backbone of effective wilderness first aid. Attend courses, practice regularly, and stay informed about the latest guidelines and techniques. First aid is a skill set that requires continuous improvement and adaptation.

The wilderness calls to the spirit of adventure in all of us. It's a place of beauty and tranquility, but also of unpredictability and danger. Knowing how to effectively manage bleeding with direct pressure and tourniquets is more than a skill—it's a duty to yourself and those who journey with you. Let this knowledge empower you to face the challenges of the wild with confidence and courage.

Embrace the responsibility of learning and mastering these lifesaving techniques. The knowledge you carry into the wilderness can make all the difference. Let it be a beacon of safety that illuminates the path for others to follow.

Shock

In the wilderness, shock can be a silent threat, looming like a shadow, ready to deepen the crisis of any injury or illness if not recognized and addressed promptly. Understanding shock in the vast expanses of the outdoors is not just about knowledge; it's about preparation, reaction, and the will to survive and help others do the same. Shock occurs when the body isn't getting enough blood flow, which can happen due to various reasons like severe blood loss, infections, allergic reactions, or significant trauma. It's crucial to recognize the signs early—such as rapid heartbeat, weak pulse, shallow breathing, cold/clammy skin, and confusion or agitation—because, in the realm of wilderness first aid, time is not a luxury one can afford to waste.

To initially manage shock, the focus should be on ensuring the victim is lying down with their legs elevated, if possible, to promote blood flow to the vital organs. Keeping them warm, calm, and still is just as vital as providing treatment for any injuries or illnesses causing the shock. Remember, your voice can be a powerful tool in combating shock; a calm, reassuring tone can provide an immense psychological boost in a situation where fear and panic are your enemies. Be swift, be decisive, and act with the confidence that the steps you're taking could save a life. In the untamed corners of our world, where nature reigns supreme, being well-versed in recognizing and treating shock isn't just a skill—it's a lifeline that can mean the difference between despair and hope, between being a victim and a survivor.

Recognition and Initial Care

In the realm of wilderness first aid, recognizing shock and delivering immediate care stand as crucial components of emergency response. The wilderness, with its unpredictability and lack of immediate professional medical help, demands a level of preparedness and resilience from each adventurer. Shock, a life-threatening condition resulting from inadequate blood flow throughout the body, can stem from a multitude of scenarios such as severe bleeding, allergic reactions, infections, burns, or significant emotional trauma.

Firstly, understanding the signs of shock is paramount. Symptoms may include cold, clammy skin, rapid but weak pulse, rapid breathing, nausea or vomiting, and a feeling of weakness or fatigue. The person might also appear anxious, confused, or lose consciousness. It is crucial for responders to assess the situation swiftly and accurately, as early detection can significantly influence the outcome.

The initial step in caring for someone in shock is to ensure their airway is clear and that they are breathing. If they are not breathing, immediate CPR may be necessary. In cases where breathing is stable, focus on controlling any bleeding by applying direct pressure to wounds, which can help prevent the condition from worsening. Remember, your actions in these moments are vital and can make a substantial difference in the patient's recovery.

Next, it is important to keep the person warm and comfortable. Shock can disrupt the body's ability to regulate temperature, leading to a dangerous drop in body heat. Use blankets or extra clothing to help retain the person's body heat. Even in warmer climates, individuals in shock can become dangerously cold.

Elevating the person's legs slightly, unless you suspect spinal injuries or broken bones, can help improve blood flow to vital organs. This simple maneuver can be instrumental in managing shock effectively. However, it's essential to exercise caution and use your best judgment based on the situation's specifics.

Reassurance is another key element in the initial care of someone experiencing shock. A calm and composed demeanor can be incredibly soothing to the patient, reducing stress and anxiety levels. Communicate clearly and let them know help is on the way. This emotional support, while it might seem small, can have a profound impact on the patient's condition.

Dehydration can exacerbate shock, so if the person is conscious and able to swallow, providing small sips of water can be beneficial. However, caution is advised if there's a risk of vomiting, as it could complicate the situation further.

One of the most challenging aspects of dealing with shock in a wilderness setting is the unpredictability and isolation. This makes it imperative to call for professional medical help as soon as possible. If you're in a remote location, use a cell phone, satellite phone, or another form of emergency communication to alert authorities. In the meantime, continue to monitor the patient's vital signs, such as their pulse and breathing rate, and be ready to provide CPR or other forms of life support if their condition deteriorates.

While waiting for help to arrive, it's essential to shield the patient from the elements to the best of your ability. Weather conditions can quickly worsen the patient's state, so seek shelter if the environment poses an additional risk. This could mean moving the patient to a shaded area, protecting them from the sun, or creating a makeshift shelter to guard against wind or rain.

Documentation plays a critical role in the effective management of shock in wilderness settings. If possible, keep a record of the patient's symptoms, any care provided, and their responses to the treatments. This information can be invaluable to professional medical personnel upon their arrival, enabling them to make informed decisions quickly.

A proactive approach to learning and preparedness can significantly mitigate the risks associated with shock. This entails not only acquiring knowledge through resources such as this book but also through practical training. Wilderness first aid courses provide hands-on experience that can be crucial in real-life situations, offering insights into managing shock and other emergencies that are difficult to gain through reading alone.

In closing, recognizing shock and knowing how to initiate care can significantly impact the outcome of a wilderness emergency. The keys to success lie in preparation, swift action, and a calm demeanor. Remember, your ability to respond effectively can make all the difference in a life-threatening situation. While the wilderness presents unique challenges, it also inspires a spirit of resilience and resourcefulness. Embrace these qualities, and let them guide you in making informed decisions that can save lives.

Let this knowledge empower you as you venture into the wild, not as a source of fear, but as a foundation of confidence and strength. The wilderness beckons with its beauty and mystery, and with the right skills, you can explore this vast expanse with the assurance that you are equipped to face whatever challenges may arise. Be bold, be cautious, and above all, be prepared. The capabilities you develop now can serve you well beyond the confines of the wilderness, enriching your adventures and ensuring that you not only survive but thrive in the great outdoors.

Chapter 7:
Fractures and Sprains

The journey into the wild is fraught with unpredictability - terrain that challenges your body and tests your limits. Within these pages, we'll delve into the crucial knowledge of recognizing and managing fractures and sprains, injuries commonly encountered in the remote embrace of nature. As adventurers, the power to heal, to support, and to persevere lies within our grasp; understanding the nuances between a fracture and a sprain sets the stage for effective first aid that can not only safeguard an expedition but also, in some cases, save a life. Mastery of **splinting techniques** is essential, allowing us to use both improvised and commercial splints, ensuring that an injured limb is immobilized with the care and precision it requires. Equally important is the skill to manage **sprains and strains**, employing the RICE technique (Rest, Ice, Compression, Elevation) to reduce swelling and mitigate pain. This chapter doesn't just offer guidelines; it serves as a beacon of knowledge, empowering you with the confidence and skills needed to face these challenges head-on. Whether the mishap is a twisted ankle on a rugged trail or a more severe fracture miles from civilization, you'll be equipped to provide the essential care that can make all the difference. Let's embark on this chapter not just as readers, but as intrepid souls ready to embrace the resilience within us, for in the wild, the strength to heal is as vital as the spirit of adventure itself.

Splinting Techniques

In the unforgiving embrace of the wilderness, where every step could pivot from adventure to emergency, mastering the art of splinting emerges as a cornerstone of preparedness. It's not just about having the skill; it's about embodying the resilience to face fractures and sprains head-on, with the confidence of a seasoned outdoor enthusiast. Splinting, an essential procedure in the realm of first aid, is pivotal in immobilizing broken limbs or sprained joints, mitigating pain, and preventing further injury. Whether you're miles deep in the forest or scaling a remote peak, understanding how to fabricate both improvised and commercial splints is your invisible shield against the unforeseen. This section dives into the heart of splinting techniques, illuminating the path to crafting effective supports from the resources at your disposal or leveraging commercial products designed for wilderness exigencies. By embracing these methods with both creativity and precision, you equip yourself with a powerful tool in emergency care—transforming challenges into tales of triumph and ensuring that every adventure, no matter how rugged, remains within the realm of safe exploration.

Improvised and Commercial Splints

Splinting in the wilderness can be a critical skill, turning a potentially dire situation into one that's manageable until professional medical help can be reached. The art of splinting, using both improvised and commercial products, is an invaluable aspect of wilderness first aid that cannot be overlooked.

When you're miles away from the nearest hospital and help may be hours, or even days away, knowing how to stabilize a fractured or sprained limb can make a significant difference in the outcome for the injured person. This is where the creativity and resourcefulness inherent in every outdoor enthusiast come into play.

Commercial splints are specifically designed for stabilizing and immobilizing injured limbs. They are lightweight, compact, and often adjustable, making them a must-have in any comprehensive wilderness first aid kit. Materials like SAM splints, which can be molded to fit any limb, are incredibly versatile and effective.

However, there will be times when you don't have access to these commercial options. In these instances, the environment around you becomes your first aid kit. Everything from branches and backpack straps to sleeping pads and clothing can be used to create an effective splint.

The primary goal of splinting is to immobilize and protect the injured limb, preventing further injury. When improvising a splint, you must ensure that the materials you choose are sturdy enough to support the limb. For a fractured arm or wrist, for instance, a straight branch bound with strips of cloth for padding and securement can serve well.

Utilizing items like trekking poles is another innovative solution. They can be tied alongside a leg with fractures to provide the necessary stabilization. Similarly, an inflatable sleeping pad can be rolled tightly around an injured limb and then secured to act as a makeshift splint, providing both immobilization and cushioning.

Remember, improvising a splint requires not just creativity, but knowledge of basic anatomy and biomechanics. The splint should always immobilize the joints above and below the injury. This principle is paramount to prevent movement and further damage.

Padding is another crucial element when constructing any splint, improvised or commercial. Padding helps to reduce pressure points, which can be particularly painful and damaging over time. Items like socks, gloves, or even leaves and moss can serve as padding in a pinch.

While the effectiveness of a splint - especially an improvised one - largely depends on the materials available and the severity of the injury, the proper technique is always the same. Stabilize the limb in the position found, ensure the splint extends beyond the joints above and below the injury, and check for circulation beyond the splint to prevent any restriction of blood flow.

Practicing these skills before you need them is invaluable. Regularly review and practice splinting techniques as part of your wilderness first aid training. This ensures that when a real-life scenario arises, you're prepared and confident in your abilities to respond effectively.

Moreover, never underestimate the psychological impact of providing first aid care, such as splinting, to someone in distress. Your ability to remain calm, collected, and confident can significantly impact the injured person's mental state, inspiring hope and a positive outlook, even in the face of adversity.

Finally, always reassess the injury after applying a splint. Check for signs of poor circulation, like numbness, tingling, or a bluish color. Ensuring that the splint is doing its job without causing additional harm is a continuous process until professional help is received.

The wilderness offers us a return to the basics and tests our resilience. Splinting, a blend of art and science, requires us to use our knowledge, skills, and environment in innovative ways. Whether using a high-tech commercial splint or branches and cloth, the goal remains the same: stabilize, protect, and support the injured limb to prevent further harm.

As you head into the wild, remember that preparation is key. Equip yourself with both the tools and the knowledge to use them effectively. Understanding the principles of splinting with both improvised and commercial materials will equip you to face unexpected challenges, ensuring that you and your companions can navigate the wilderness with confidence and safety.

In conclusion, whether you're dealing with a minor sprain on a day hike or a more serious fracture in a remote backcountry setting, the principles of splinting remain a cornerstone of wilderness first aid. By mastering these skills, you become not just a more competent adventurer but a guardian of those who venture with you into the great outdoors. Let's embrace the challenges of the wilderness with the knowledge and skills to safeguard ourselves and others.

Managing Sprains and Strains

In the wilderness, where each step on uneven terrain carries the risk of injury, understanding how to manage sprains and strains can be the difference between a minor inconvenience and a trip-ending ordeal. The cornerstone of treating these injuries is the RICE technique: Rest, Ice, Compression, Elevation. It's a strategy as fundamental to wilderness first aid as staying calm is to survival. The first step, Rest, isn't just about stopping the activity that caused the injury; it's about preserving your ability to continue your adventure tomorrow. Ice, often scarce in the wild, demands ingenuity – cold streams or snow-packed in a barrier can serve in a pinch. Compression and Elevation aren't just treatments; they're a language your body understands, a way to communicate that it's time to heal. As adventurers and stewards of the wild, we're reminded that our greatest tool isn't the gear in our pack but the knowledge in our minds. Harnessing the simple power of the RICE technique equips us to face adversity, not with fear, but with the confidence and resilience that define the spirit of exploration.

RICE Technique (Rest, Ice, Compression, Elevation)

In the wilderness, where every action and reaction is magnified by the isolation and rawness of nature, understanding how to swiftly and effectively respond to injuries is paramount. For adventurers, outdoor enthusiasts, and professionals in remote areas, mastering the RICE technique presents a vital skill set in managing sprains and strains. This simple yet profoundly effective approach can significantly influence the outcome of an injury, turning what might have been a major impediment into a manageable inconvenience.

Let's delve into the first component, **Rest**. When you're miles away from the nearest clinic or hospital, resting might not seem like the most proactive advice. However, resting is crucial in the initial hours after an injury. It prevents further damage and starts the healing process on the right foot. This does not mean you must halt all movement but rather avoid putting weight or strain on the injured area. For wilderness explorers, this could mean setting up camp earlier than planned or adjusting your pack to redistribute weight away from the injured limb.

Moving onto **Ice**, which can sometimes be a logistical challenge in outdoor settings. Yet, its importance cannot be overstated. Ice reduces swelling and numbs the pain, creating conditions that can vastly improve recovery times. When ice isn't readily available, cold streams or snowpacks serve as excellent natural substitutes. Insulate the skin with a barrier, such as cloth or a piece of clothing, to prevent frostbite, then apply the cold source for short periods.

The third principle, **Compression**, involves snugly wrapping the injured area to prevent excessive swelling, which can further damage. This method does not require specialized equipment – a bandana, scarf, or even a clean sock can be used to gently wrap the injury. The key is to apply enough pressure to support the area without hindering circulation.

Elevation, the final element, leverages gravity to control swelling and aid in the removal of waste products from the injured area. By keeping the injury at or above heart level whenever possible, you enhance the healing process. This might mean getting creative with backpacks and gear to prop up an injured leg or finding a natural incline to rest an arm.

It's vital to recognize the signs that indicate a more serious injury, necessitating professional medical attention. Persistent swelling, discoloration, inability to bear weight, or severe pain when moving the area are red flags. Wilderness first aid is about stabilization and management; it's not a substitute for professional care when it's truly needed.

Integrating the RICE technique into your wilderness first aid repertoire empowers you to mitigate injuries swiftly and effectively, ensuring they don't escalate into more significant issues. This knowledge engenders a sense of confidence and resilience, traits that are invaluable when facing the unpredictability of nature.

This technique is not a one-size-fits-all solution, and its application may vary based on the individual's condition and the specific circumstances of the injury. Being adaptable and resourceful, improvising with the materials at hand, and using sound judgment can make all the difference in the effective use of RICE in the wilderness.

At its core, RICE is not merely a set of actions but a mindset. It embodies the principles of wilderness first aid: prevention, preparedness, and swift, effective response. These principles don't just apply to physical challenges; they're reflective of the larger ethos of wilderness exploration. Every adventurer knows that adaptability, resilience, and knowledge are their best tools when venturing into the great outdoors.

Understanding and applying the RICE technique can make the crucial difference in how you manage potential injuries, influencing not just your immediate comfort but your overall wilderness experience. It's about minimizing impact, ensuring safety, and preserving the ability to embark on future adventures.

The wilderness calls to different people for different reasons. For some, it's the thrill of exploration, for others, the beauty of solitude. Whatever your call to the wild, knowing how to care for yourself and others in the face of injury is a responsibility that comes with stepping off the beaten path.

Aspiring to be prepared is not about expecting the worst but about embracing the freedom that comes with self-reliance. The more adept you are at managing potential setbacks like sprains and strains, the more confidently you can immerse yourself in the adventure, secure in the knowledge that you are equipped to handle what comes your way.

In conclusion, the RICE technique is an essential component of wilderness first aid that stands as testament to the power of simple, informed actions in the face of adversity. Its principles of Rest, Ice, Compression, and Elevation are not just steps to be followed but are pillars of a holistic approach to managing injuries in remote environments.

Embrace this knowledge, integrate these practices into your wilderness readiness toolkit, and carry them with you as you venture forth into the wild. Your adventures await, and with the confidence that comes from being prepared, you're set to meet them head-on, come what may.

Chapter 8: Water Safety and Drowning Prevention

Embarking on adventures near or on the water brings a tranquility and exhilaration that's hard to match. Yet, for all its beauty, water poses unique risks that demand our respect and preparedness. This chapter delves into the critical aspects of water safety and drowning prevention, empowering outdoor enthusiasts with the knowledge to not only recognize the signs of drowning but also execute rescue techniques that could save a life. It's a sobering reality that many drowning incidents are preventable, and being equipped with the right skills and understanding can transform outcomes. We'll explore everything from identifying distress in the water to performing safe and effective rescues. By adopting a mindset of vigilance and responsibility, you, as an adventurer, can ensure that your water-related activities are not only enjoyable but also secure. Remember, the mastery of these techniques is not just for your safety but could also enable you to be a lifeline for others. Water, with all its majesty, should never be underestimated. Moving through this chapter, you'll gain not just the skills but also the confidence to face water hazards with the courage and preparedness they necessitate.

Recognizing Drowning

In the expansive realm of water safety and drowning prevention, understanding the real-life, often subtle signs of drowning is vital for outdoor adventurers, campers, hikers, and professionals working in remote areas. Unlike the dramatic portrayals in films and media, real drowning is quiet and can happen astonishingly quickly. It's imperative to recognize that drowning individuals often can't signal for help or make a sound; their bodies are instead focused on trying to breathe. Look for signs such as the person's mouth at water level, unable to keep it consistently above surface, attempts to swim without making progress, or having their head tilted back with mouth open in an effort to breathe. Their arms might be laterally extended or pressing down on the water's surface in a bid to lift themselves up. By equipping yourself with the knowledge to identify these critical signs, you're positioning yourself as a lifeline, capable of transforming a potential tragedy into a tale of resilience and survival. Your courage to learn and apply drowning recognition can be the beacon of hope amidst the waves of uncertainty, ensuring safety and instilling confidence within your group and yourself when facing the unpredictability of wild waters.

Signs and Symptoms of Drowning

When we venture into the great outdoors, embracing the thrills of water-based activities, it's crucial to be armed with the knowledge that can tip the balance between a minor mishap and a life-threatening situation. Recognizing the signs and symptoms of drowning is a cornerstone of wilderness safety, empowering us to act swiftly and decisively in the face of danger.

Drowning, contrary to popular belief, does not always involve loud cries for help or dramatic splashing. In reality, it's often a silent struggle, making it imperative to understand the more subtle indicators of someone in distress. One of the hallmark signs of drowning is the victim's inability to call out for help, as their primary focus is on breathing rather than speaking. This crucial fact highlights the silent nature of most drowning incidents, underscoring the importance of vigilant supervision.

Another significant symptom is the victim's body position in the water. Individuals who are drowning frequently appear to be climbing an invisible ladder, with their arms moving laterally while they try to push down on the water to lift their mouths out of the water for air. This movement is starkly different from regular swimming motions, where arms are typically used to pull the body forward.

The victim's facial expressions can also offer vital clues. A look of panic, wide-eyed with a gaping or closed mouth, is common when someone is fighting to stay afloat. This expression of distress, while perhaps subtle from a distance, is a powerful call to action for those familiar with drowning's insidious nature.

A person who is drowning may struggle to maintain their head above water, often tipping backward, with their mouth at water level. This precarious position prevents effective breathing, signaling a dire need for immediate assistance. The alternating submerging and reappearing of the head is a critical visual cue that should prompt an immediate response.

Evidence of a drowning event isn't solely confined to the person's movements or facial expressions. The lack of expected noise, like the absence of splashing or verbal cues, can be a significant indicator. Drowning victims are frequently unable to wave for help since their instinctual response is to utilize their hands to press against the water's surface to lift their bodies for air, leaving them helpless to signal to others visually.

In cases involving children, a sudden silence is a potent warning sign, especially if the child was previously vocal. Kids playing in the water are naturally noisy, so silence might indicate that they can't keep their head above water to speak or breathe.

Furthermore, drowning can occur in a variety of conditions - from deep water to unexpectedly shallow areas where individuals might feel a false sense of security. Even proficient swimmers are at risk under certain circumstances, such as being caught in an undertow or experiencing a cramp. Recognizing distress signals in all types of water environments is essential for timely intervention.

Efforts to reach or cling to a floatation device in a desperate manner can also suggest someone is in trouble. While this might seem like an apparent sign, it's often overlooked as onlookers may misinterpret desperate grasping for playful splashing around.

The timeline for rescuing a drowning victim is incredibly short. Brain damage and fatal outcomes can occur within minutes after oxygen supply is cut off. This narrow window emphasizes the necessity for rapid recognition and action. Being prepared to recognize the early signs of drowning and respond appropriately can make all the difference.

Equipping ourselves with the knowledge of these symptoms acts as the first line of defense against drowning. Awareness allows us to maintain a proactive stance, ready to spring into action at the slightest indication of trouble. This informed vigilance is particularly vital in wilderness settings, where immediate professional help is not always at hand.

In summary, the signs and symptoms of drowning demand our undivided attention and a nuanced understanding of their silent nature. As lovers of the outdoors and guardians of our fellow adventurers, embracing this knowledge positions us as crucial sentinels against the deceptive calm of aquatic perils.

Let this awareness inspire a commitment to safety that matches our passion for exploration. By keeping watch over one another with informed eyes, we not only protect lives but also nurture the spirit of adventure that draws us to the wilderness. Remember, your knowledge and vigilance can be the lifeline that turns a potential tragedy into a tale of survival and resilience.

Embrace this responsibility with the gravity it deserves. Let the knowledge of signs and symptoms of drowning guide your actions and interventions, transforming you into a beacon of safety in the unpredictable wilderness of water. Your preparedness and foresight can make all the difference in the world, potentially saving a life and ensuring that the beauty of the great outdoors remains a source of joy, not tragedy.

Rescue Techniques

In the woven tapestry of wilderness safety, the art of rescue is not just about bravery but about knowledge, skill, and the judicious use of both. Whether you're faced with a serene lake that suddenly betrays with an undercurrent or a deceptive stream that ensnares with its icy grip, understanding the right rescue techniques can mean the difference between life and despair. The cornerstone of any water rescue is the principle of 'reach or throw, don't go', ensuring that your own safety remains paramount. If the situation escalates and a direct approach is inevitable, it's crucial to utilize techniques that minimize risk—like approaching from behind to avoid a panic-stricken grasp. Once secured, your initial care sets the stage for survival, emphasizing gentle re-warming and reassurance while avoiding actions that could aggravate a potential spinal injury. This section, rich with strategies and insights, empowers you to stand on the shore of uncertainty and act with confidence, melding the will to save with the wisdom to do it wisely. As you immerse yourself in these pages, remember: the heart of a rescuer beats with the courage to act and the conviction to change the ending of what could have been a tragic tale.

Safe Rescue and Initial Care

Transitioning smoothly from the methodical steps of recognizing the signs of drowning, we now venture into the critical actions of safe rescue and initial care. The essence of wilderness first aid and emergency response is not just about having the technical skills; it's about applying those skills under pressure, with compassion, and with the ultimate goal of preserving life.

In the wilderness, every second matters during a rescue operation. Initiating a safe rescue is paramount; rushing in without assessing the situation can lead to further harm. Remember, the safety of the rescuer takes precedence. If the situation is too perilous, it's crucial to seek professional help rather than risking multiple lives.

Upon ensuring a safe approach, if the victim is unconscious or unable to swim, it's essential to approach them from behind to avoid a panicky reaction that could endanger both the rescuer and the victim. Use a calm, assertive voice to reassure the victim as you guide them to safety. Training in water rescue techniques is invaluable, providing the skills to approach and secure the victim effectively without causing further distress or injury.

Once on solid ground, the initial care begins with assessing the victim's airway, breathing, and circulation—ABCs. Is the person breathing? Do they have a pulse? These are the critical questions that need swift answers. If the person is not breathing, is gasping for air, or has no pulse, immediate CPR may be necessary, adhering to the latest guidelines and recommendations.

After addressing the immediate dangers of drowning, hypothermia is the next concern, especially in cold water incidents. The goal is to gently warm the victim, avoiding any rapid rewarming methods that could lead to shock. Wrap them in blankets, use your own body heat, or employ emergency thermal blankets if available. Every bit of warmth matters.

It's also imperative to closely monitor the person for any signs of delayed drowning, a rare but serious condition where water enters the lungs, causing difficulties breathing. Symptoms can manifest hours after the rescue, underscoring the importance of obtaining medical evaluation and monitoring even after a seemingly successful rescue.

The mental state of the person rescued is another aspect that warrants attention. Experiencing a near-drowning event can be traumatic. Exhibiting calmness, reassurance, and empathy can significantly impact their psychological recovery. Engage in simple, reassuring conversations, avoid overstimulation, and let them know help is on the way.

Efficient communication with emergency services is crucial. Provide them with precise information about the location, condition of the victim, and any first aid actions already taken. Knowledge of the wilderness area and preparation, including maps and GPS devices, aids significantly in expediting the arrival of professional help.

The role of bystanders can't be overstated. Enlisting the help of others to signal for help, gather resources, or provide emotional support to the victim enhances the efficiency of the rescue operation. Teamwork is often the backbone of successful wilderness rescues.

Understanding and recognizing the risks associated with water bodies in wilderness settings are critical. Educating oneself and others about these dangers, preventive measures, and safe rescue techniques can significantly reduce the number of water-related emergencies. Prevention is always preferable to the need for rescue.

Continuing education and practice in water safety, swimming, and first aid ensures that your skills remain sharp and you're prepared for emergencies. Engaging in regular training exercises, attending workshops, and refreshing your knowledge plays a pivotal role in being an effective rescuer.

Maintaining a well-stocked first aid kit tailored for water safety is another essential aspect of preparedness. Including items specific for treating hypothermia, water inhalation, and minor injuries can make a significant difference in the outcome of a rescue situation.

Advocacy for wearing life jackets and implementing safe swimming practices should not be underestimated. Encouraging these behaviors in others, especially in children, fosters a culture of safety and awareness around water bodies.

In closing, the spirit of wilderness adventure should always be balanced with respect for nature's power and unpredictability. By equipping oneself with the knowledge and skills for safe rescue and initial care, you not only protect yourself and your fellow adventurers but also honor the wilderness you seek to explore. Let us cherish and preserve the very adventures that call us to the wild, ensuring that our stories are ones of inspiration, safety, and respect for all elements of nature.

Chapter 9:
Wilderness Survival Skills

In the tapestry of wilderness adventures, the thread of survival skills weaves through every moment, empowering you to face the unknown with confidence and capability. As we delve into the essentials of building shelters and sourcing water and food, your toolkit for thriving in the great outdoors will expand, illustrating that with the right knowledge, the wild isn't an adversary but an invitation to discover resilience you may not have known you possessed. Building shelters is not just about protection; it's an art form that connects us with the wisdom of those who navigated these landscapes long before us. You'll learn not just the mechanics but the principles behind various types of shelters, ensuring you can adapt to any environment. When it comes to water and food, the lesson is clear: nature provides, but wisdom discerns. Identifying safe sources of hydration and sustenance is a skill that pays homage to the symbiotic relationship we share with the earth. Every sip of water and bite of food becomes a testament to the informed decisions and respect we carry into the wilderness. With every chapter, remember, these aren't just skills; they're a dialogue with nature, a step toward self-reliance, and a journey into the heart of what it means to truly live in the rhythm of the natural world.

Building Shelters

In your journey to mastering wilderness survival skills, understanding the art of building shelters stands as a cornerstone. It's not just about finding refuge from the harsh elements; it's about creating a haven that can significantly increase your chances of survival. Whether faced with the biting cold or sweltering heat, the right shelter can make all the difference. There are various types and techniques to shelter building - from lean-tos and A-frames to snow caves and natural shelters. But it's not merely the structure that matters; it's about leveraging the resources around you, understanding the environment you're in, and applying that knowledge with precision and creativity. Each situation may call for a different type of shelter, and mastering these skills requires practice, patience, and persistence. The goal is to ensure that, no matter where you find yourself, you're equipped with the knowledge to protect yourself and others from the elements. This section is a testament to the power of adaptation and resilience, aiming to inspire confidence and competence in building life-saving shelters in the wilderness.

Types and Techniques

The Types and Techniques of building shelters in the wilderness are skills that lie at the heart of survival. Venturing into the great outdoors brings with it a sense of freedom and adventure. Yet, it's this very freedom that introduces an element of unpredictability, often throwing challenges your way that require more than just a basic knowledge of survival—they demand creativity, resilience, and an understanding of the environment around you.

The first type often taught to outdoor enthusiasts is the 'lean-to' shelter. Made by leaning branches or logs against a horizontal support, such as a fallen tree or a sturdy branch wedged between two trees, this structure provides a basic cover from elements. The orientation of your lean-to is crucial; always have the back facing the prevailing wind for maximum protection. Adding foliage to the top can further insulate and shield you from rain or snow.

Another vital technique is the creation of a 'debris hut,' which can be a lifesaver in cold environments. This shelter uses a frame of branches covered with leaves, moss, or any other available debris to create insulation. The principle behind the debris hut is simple—maximize warmth and minimize exposure. The small space inside reduces the area your body needs to heat, essential in conserving energy in a survival situation.

For those in snowy climates, the 'snow cave' or 'quinzee' can be a remarkable form of shelter. By piling snow into a mound and allowing it to sinter, or slightly melt and refreeze, you can carve out a hollow interior that traps body heat and blocks the wind. However, it's essential to ensure adequate ventilation to prevent carbon monoxide buildup, a detail that underlines the importance of knowledge and caution in survival techniques.

Not all shelter-building endeavors require elaboration; sometimes, simplicity is key. The 'tarp shelter' is a testament to this, demonstrating how a well-positioned tarp and some paracord can create an effective barrier against precipitation and wind. The versatility of the tarp shelter means it can be pitched in various configurations, tailored to the specific needs of the site and weather conditions.

In tropical or bug-infested areas, the 'hammock shelter' becomes invaluable. Suspended off the ground, it protects against ground-dwelling insects, snakes, and wet soil. Integrating a mosquito net and a rainfly transforms this resting place into a formidable outdoor sleeping solution.

The concept of an 'igloo' is traditional yet fascinating, offering an excellent example of using available resources—snow, in this instance—to create an efficient shelter. The blocks used to construct an igloo are cut from snow that has been compacted by the wind, providing structural stability and insulation. Building an igloo requires skill and understanding of snow properties, making it an advanced technique.

Creating effective wilderness shelters is not merely about following instructions; it's about adapting to your environment. The 'natural shelter' method epitomizes this. Caves, rock overhangs, or even dense foliage can offer immediate protection without the need for extensive construction. However, always be cautious of existing occupants, such as wildlife, that may view your chosen spot as their home.

Adaptability extends to 'improvised shelters' as well. Every outdoor adventure is different, and sometimes, you must work with what you have. It could be as simple as using a canoe and paddles to form the skeleton of a shelter, covered with whatever materials are at hand. The key principle here is resourcefulness—the ability to look at your surroundings and see not just what is there, but what could be.

When constructing any shelter, the 'location' is a factor that cannot be overstressed. A good shelter in the wrong place—for example, in a dry riverbed prone to flash flooding or under a lone tree during a thunderstorm—can lead to disaster. Always assess the terrain, considering factors such as water proximity, potential hazards, and exposure to elements before deciding on a site.

Much like the diversity of shelters, the 'techniques' used in their construction are numerous. Basic knot-tying skills can turn a piece of rope into a pivotal tool, whether in lashing branches together for a frame or securing a tarp. The ability to use nature's offerings, such as weaving foliage into a mat or crafting wooden stakes with a knife, demonstrates that the art of shelter-building is as much about technique as it is about materials.

Emphasizing the 'practice' aspect cannot be underestimated. Learning about different types of shelters is one thing; building them is another. Regular practice in varied environments hones your skills, teaches you the limitations and potential of materials, and prepares you for the unexpected. After all, in a real survival situation, your hands and knowledge are your best tools.

Yet, building shelters is more than just a survival skill—it's an act that connects us with our ancestors, who lived in harmony with nature, understanding its rhythms and respecting its power. In every branch woven into the walls of a debris hut, or snow block carved for an igloo, there's a reminder of the human spirit's resilience and creativity.

In essence, the types and techniques of building wilderness shelters are about much more than physical structures. They embody preparation, adaptability, and the art of seeing not just what is, but what can be. They remind us that, even in the most challenging circumstances, we have the capacity to create safety, warmth, and refuge with our own two hands.

As you venture into the wilderness, let the knowledge of these shelters be not just a tool for survival, but a bridge to the past and a testament to your ability to thrive in harmony with the natural world. This mastery isn't just a tribute to human ingenuity; it's a profound connection to the earth that sustains us. Wherever you find yourselves under the vast, unforgiving sky, remember—you have the power to make it home, even if only for a night.

Finding Water and Food

In the vast embrace of the wilderness, your survival hinges not just on sheer will, but on the practical skills you possess—among them, the crucial ability to find water and food. The quest for hydration should guide you to seek out natural water sources, such as streams, rivers, or even morning dew, emphasizing the paramount importance of purification before consumption to avoid illness. Meanwhile, food procurement, though secondary to water, requires a keen understanding of the environment to identify edible plants, insects, and, if necessary, methods for trapping or fishing. Mastery of these skills can transform the daunting wilderness into a landscape of potential sustenance. Remember, nature isn't against you; with the right knowledge, it becomes your ally in survival. Embracing this mindset can significantly elevate your confidence and capability in navigating the challenges of finding water and food in the wild. This journey of self-reliance not only tests your limits but expands them, proving that with persistence and the right skills, thriving in the wilderness is within your reach.

Safe Sources and Preparation

In the heart of the wilderness, where the embrace of nature is both a blessing and a challenge, finding safe water and food can become a paramount task. It's not just about survival; it's about thriving in an environment that demands respect, preparation, and knowledge. For outdoor enthusiasts, adventurers, and those who find themselves in remote areas, understanding how to secure safe sources of water and food, and knowing the correct methods of preparation, can make all the difference.

When it comes to water, the source is as important as the treatment. Streams, rivers, and lakes may seem like abundant sources, but they can also be teeming with pathogens that are invisible to the naked eye. Boiling is a reliable method to purify water, killing bacteria, viruses, and parasites. A rolling boil for at least one minute (or three minutes at altitudes above 6,500 feet) is considered effective. However, when a heat source is not available, chemical purifiers such as iodine or chlorine dioxide can be viable alternatives, as long as they're used according to the manufacturer's instructions.

The allure of the wilderness also brings the necessity of finding food. Edible plants can provide vital nutrients, but the golden rule is never to eat any plant unless you are 100% certain of its identification and safety. Many plants are poisonous and can look similar to edible ones. Investing time in learning about local flora from reliable sources before your journey can save you from a dangerous mistake. Foraging guides specific to the region you're exploring are invaluable resources.

For those who fish or hunt during their wilderness adventures, understanding the principles of safe preparation and cooking is crucial. Fish and game must be cooked thoroughly to avoid foodborne illnesses. A food thermometer can be a great addition to your wilderness toolkit, ensuring that fish and meats reach a safe internal temperature; for most game, this is at least 160°F (71°C).

Packing non-perishable food items is also a wise strategy. High-energy, lightweight, and durable items such as nuts, seeds, dried fruits, and energy bars can supplement foraged or hunted food. These items don't require preparation, making them immediate sources of energy and nutrition.

Conservation is another critical aspect. Take only what you need from nature and utilize all parts of any plants or animals you harvest. This respect for the environment not only sustains its abundance but also deepens your connection to the wild.

The importance of safe food storage in the wilderness cannot be overstated. Proper storage techniques protect your food from wildlife and help preserve the natural behaviors of animals. Using bear-proof containers and hanging food bags well away from your campsite are practices that promote safety for both adventurers and animals.

Hydration plays a pivotal role in wilderness survival. Carrying a durable water filter or purifying tablets can make most water sources safe to drink. It's essential to hydrate regularly, not just when you feel thirsty, to maintain optimal energy levels and physical function.

Emergency preparedness should include knowing how to ration food and water without compromising your health. In situations where supplies are limited, prioritizing hydration over food is vital, as the human body can survive longer without food than it can without water.

Understanding the signs of food and waterborne illnesses is part of being well-prepared. Symptoms like nausea, vomiting, diarrhea, and fever can quickly lead to dehydration and require immediate attention, especially in remote settings.

Planning your route with potential natural water sources in mind can help manage your water supply more effectively. Be sure to document these on your map and have a clear plan for reaching each source.

The practice of leaving no trace should extend to your food and water sourcing. Collect water and harvest food in a way that minimizes impact on the ecosystem, ensuring that future visitors and inhabitants can enjoy the same resources.

Invest in quality gear designed for wilderness use, such as lightweight, compact, and durable cooking equipment. Gear that's easy to pack and carry enhances your ability to prepare food safely and efficiently.

Finally, embrace the learning opportunities that come with preparing food and water in the wilderness. Each experience enriches your skills and deepens your appreciation for the natural world. It's a process of continuous learning and adaptation.

By being informed, prepared, and respectful, you can safely enjoy the bounty that nature offers. The wilderness provides an extraordinary classroom, teaching lessons of self-reliance, sustainability, and the interconnectivity of life. Whether you're an experienced adventurer or new to wilderness exploration, the principles of safe sources and preparation are fundamental to the journey. Let the wilderness inspire you, but also remember that with the privilege of exploring it comes the responsibility to protect it, ensuring it remains a resource and refuge for generations to come.

Chapter 10: Navigating Common Health Issues

In the journey of wilderness exploration, familiarizing oneself with the management of common health issues becomes as crucial as mastering the terrain. As adventurers, we often prepare for the immediate threats—those that lash out with fangs or hide in the cold shadows—but it's the silent battles, those against one's own body, that can turn the tide of survival. This chapter delves into the art of handling ubiquitous health concerns such as allergies, where the prompt use of an EpiPen could mean the difference between life and breathless silence. It journeys further into the management of chronic conditions like diabetes and asthma, offering a blueprint for maintaining control when your body's inner workings become unpredictable adversaries. Understanding the nuances of these conditions prepares you not just to survive, but to thrive in the wilderness, transforming challenges into testimonies of resilience. Embrace this knowledge as your ally; let it fortify your resolve as you embark on adventures, knowing that your preparation extends beyond the pack on your back. It's about whole-being readiness—mind, body, and spirit—geared towards conquering not just the external wilderness, but the internal frontiers where true exploration begins.

Dealing with Allergies

When you're miles away from the nearest hospital, and the wilderness is your closest companion, understanding how to manage allergies can be as crucial as finding your way back to civilization. Allergies, whether mild or life-threatening, don't take a break just because you're exploring the great outdoors. It's about being prepared, vigilant, and ready to act. Carrying an EpiPen and knowing how to use it could mean the difference between life and death for someone with severe allergies. It's not just about preventing an unfortunate reaction; it's about embodying the resilience and preparedness that adventure demands. Remember, knowledge is a tool just as vital as your compass or map. Being well-informed about your or your companions' allergic reactions and how to swiftly manage them turns potential crises into manageable situations. It's about not letting your guard down and ensuring everyone can enjoy the wilderness safely, with confidence, and embrace the freedom it offers without the shadow of fear cast by unmanaged allergies.

EpiPen Usage

In the grand adventure of the outdoors, where the horizon stretches far beyond the reach of city lights and the air fills with the untamed spirit of nature, there lies a critical skill set that every adventurer, hiker, and wilderness professional should master: the use of an EpiPen. For individuals with severe allergies, this knowledge isn't just valuable—it's lifesaving. In these moments, you become the hero of your own story, capable of safeguarding not only your life but the lives of those around you.

The wilderness does not discriminate, and neither do allergies. They can strike swiftly and without warning, turning a serene setting into a battleground for survival. This section is dedicated to equipping you with the knowledge and confidence needed to employ an EpiPen effectively in the face of an allergic emergency. It's about transforming fear into action, ensuring that when nature calls, you're ready to answer with determination and skill.

Understanding when to use an EpiPen is the first critical step. Anaphylaxis, a severe, life-threatening allergic reaction can manifest through difficulty breathing, hives, swelling, a fast heartbeat, and dizziness among other symptoms. Recognizing these symptoms is pivotal. It's the moment where understanding transcends into action, where you reach into your first aid kit, not with hesitation, but with the assurance of someone prepared to confront the challenge head-on.

The technique of administering an EpiPen is straightforward, yet each step is crucial. Begin by removing the EpiPen from its protective case. Hold it in your fist without touching either end, as one end contains the needle, and the other, a safety release. This moment is about precision under pressure, finding calmness in the urgency.

Next, remove the safety cap, which is usually blue, to reveal the needle end. Find the outer thigh, the recommended site for injection, and ready yourself. There's no room for hesitation here. Your resolve becomes your strength. Then, in a swift motion, press the EpiPen firmly against the thigh, until you hear or feel a click, signaling that the injection has initiated.

Hold the EpiPen in place for three seconds, counting slowly. These moments are brief, yet they are the bridge from peril back to safety. Once administered, carefully remove the EpiPen and massage the injection site for about 10 seconds to aid in the absorption of the medication. Safety and care in every action, every touch.

It's crucial now more than ever to seek medical help immediately after using the EpiPen. While the epinephrine acts swiftly to counter the allergic reaction, it's not a cure; emergency medical care is essential to ensure the wellbeing of the individual. This is where communication and emergency planning, topics covered previously, become lifesavers in their own right.

Surviving the Wild

Caring for your EpiPen is just as important as knowing how to use it. Keep it in its protective case, away from extreme temperatures. It's a tool of survival, deserving respect and attention. Check it regularly to ensure it hasn't expired and that the solution inside is clear, not cloudy or discolored. Preparedness is not just about having the right tools but ensuring they're ready when you need them.

For those without known allergies, learning to use an EpiPen might seem unnecessary, yet the wilderness is unpredictable. Allergies can be discovered in the least expected moments, and being equipped with the knowledge to use an EpiPen can make you a lifeline for others. It's about extending the hand of safety and care to those around you, embodying the spirit of communal strength and preparedness.

Practice is paramount. While reading about how to use an EpiPen is a start, physical practice (with a trainer EpiPen, if possible) builds muscle memory, turning knowledge into instinct. In the throes of an emergency, your actions can become as natural as breathing, where saving a life is not just possible but probable.

Carrying an EpiPen in your wilderness first aid kit is a testament to your readiness to face the unpredictability of the outdoors head-on. It's a statement of preparedness, a commitment to life and safety, echoing the ethos of those who not only seek adventure but embrace the responsibility that comes with it.

Moreover, educating your fellow adventurers on the use of an EpiPen fosters a culture of safety and support. It transforms individual knowledge into collective wisdom, ensuring that everyone is better prepared to help each other in times of need. It's about building a community of guardians, capable and ready to stand up against the challenges of the wild.

In this journey through the wilderness of both nature and human resilience, the use of an EpiPen stands as a beacon of hope and empowerment. It exemplifies the strength found in knowledge, the courage in action, and the profound respect for life in all its fragility and unpredictability. This section is more than just instructions on using a medical device; it's a call to embrace the power within you, the power to save lives, to confront the unknown with confidence, and to walk the path less traveled with the assurance that you are never truly alone when you are prepared.

The wilderness beckons with its untamed beauty and inherent risks, inviting you to step into a world where you have the power to make a difference. Armed with the knowledge of EpiPen usage, you become a steward of the wild, a guardian of life. You step forward not with trepidation, but with the unwavering belief in your ability to turn the tide in the face of adversity. The wild calls, and with knowledge, preparation, and courage as your allies, you are ready to answer.

In summary, the mastery of EpiPen usage is more than a skill—it's a declaration of readiness, a commitment to life, and a testament to the human spirit's resilience. As you traverse the magnificent yet unpredictable terrains of our world, let this knowledge empower you, knowing that you possess the capability to face challenges with confidence and emerge victorious. Carry this wisdom as your armor, and walk the path of adventure not just as an enthusiast of the wilderness, but as a protector of life itself.

Managing Chronic Conditions in the Wilderness

Adventuring in the great outdoors presents a unique set of challenges, particularly for those managing chronic conditions such as diabetes or asthma. However, having a chronic condition shouldn't deter you from exploring the wilderness; it simply means being more prepared. First, understanding your condition inside and out is crucial—know how various situations might affect your health and what precautions you need to take. For instance, those with diabetes should monitor their blood sugar levels more frequently to prevent hypoglycemia, especially during increased physical activity. Carry a detailed medical ID and an action plan in case of an emergency, ensuring anyone who might need to help is aware of your condition and knows what to do. Also, pack extra medication and keep it in a waterproof and easily accessible container. Adapt your wilderness first aid kit to include specific supplies related to your condition, such as a spare inhaler for asthma or insulin supplies for diabetes.

Remember, the key to thriving in the wilderness with a chronic condition lies in preparation and awareness. Equip yourself with knowledge, plan meticulously, and you'll empower yourself to face the challenges of the wild head-on. Adventure awaits, and your chronic condition doesn't have to hold you back from experiencing the profound beauty and transformation that come from stepping outside your comfort zone and into nature's embrace.

Diabetes, Asthma, and Others

In the vast theatre of the wilderness, health conditions don't pause at the edge of the forest or halt at the base of the mountain. For those living with chronic conditions such as diabetes and asthma, preparation is key, not just a suggestion. Embarking on a wilderness adventure means understanding and anticipating the unique challenges these conditions may present when you're miles from the nearest road or hospital.

Managing diabetes in the wild starts with meticulous planning. Ensure you pack enough medication for the duration of your trip, plus a little extra, considering unforeseen delays. A waterproof and crush-proof container can safeguard your insulin or oral medications from the elements. Blood glucose monitoring is more critical than ever in the wilderness, where physical exertion may differ drastically from your daily routine. Frequent checks will help prevent hypo- or hyperglycemic episodes, which could swiftly turn a breathtaking hike into an emergency situation.

Asthma, much like diabetes, requires preemptive action. The key to managing asthma in remote settings lies in recognizing potential triggers and planning accordingly. Extra inhalers, spacer devices if you use them, and a course of oral corticosteroids prescribed by your doctor for flare-ups should find a place in your pack. Be mindful of pollen, cold air, and physical exertion as triggers. Establishing a breathing zone, free from campfire smoke and other irritants, can help prevent nocturnal symptoms that might otherwise escalate silently.

Adventure doesn't discriminate, and neither do chronic conditions. According to the Centers for Disease Control and Prevention (CDC), millions of Americans live with chronic diseases that could affect their ability to enjoy outdoor activities. But knowledge, preparation, and self-awareness make these barriers surmountable. By understanding your body's needs and response to various external stimuli, you can embrace the wilderness with confidence.

Beyond diabetes and asthma, many other conditions warrant special consideration. Heart disease, epilepsy, high blood pressure, and mental health conditions such as anxiety and depression are but a few examples. For those with heart conditions, a consultation with a healthcare provider before departure is essential. Activities should be matched with your level of fitness, and emergency medications like nitroglycerin should be accessible at all times.

Epilepsy poses its unique set of challenges, particularly around water safety and the potential for injury during a seizure. Informing your travel companions about your condition and educating them on how to assist in the event of a seizure can make a significant difference. Wearing a medical ID bracelet can expedite emergency care should you become unable to communicate your needs.

High blood pressure deserves attention, too. Ensure that you have a sufficient supply of medication, and monitor your blood pressure as recommended by your physician. Altitude, exertion, and dehydration can affect your blood pressure, so stay hydrated, monitor your exertion levels, and acclimate to high altitudes gradually.

Discussing mental health in the context of wilderness adventure is equally critical. The clarity and solitude of nature can be healing, yet the stress of unexpected situations or the anxiety triggered by specific environments can exacerbate existing conditions. A solid support system, whether through companions who understand your needs or through maintaining communication capabilities with loved ones, can be invaluable.

An inspirational aspect of venturing into the wild with a chronic condition is the profound sense of achievement it can bring. Each step taken is a testament to your resilience, a call to embrace the unpredictable nature of existence itself. It is about transforming limitations into chapters of a grand adventure, each challenge a dragon to be faced on your journey.

Embracing the wilderness requires not only courage but also wisdom. Wisdom to know your limits, to plan with meticulous detail, to prepare for the unexpected. The wilderness does not adapt to us; we must adapt to it, bending like the boughs of the ancient trees that whisper stories of survival in the silent forests.

The beauty of the wild calls to everyone, regardless of the invisible battles they may be fighting internally. It offers a unique canvas upon which to paint our triumphs and failures, a boundless space where the human spirit can engage with the primal forces of nature.

Every person's experience with managing chronic conditions in the wilderness will differ, much like the landscapes that stretch out before us. Sharing these experiences can not only provide practical advice but also inspire others to explore their boundaries and seek adventure, regardless of the challenges they may face. In this shared narrative, we find not only community but also the collective strength to venture beyond the familiar.

In conclusion, managing chronic conditions such as diabetes and asthma in the wilderness is both an art and a science. It requires an intimate understanding of one's body, an unwavering commitment to preparation, and an indomitable spirit willing to face the challenges head-on. The wilderness offers a unique opportunity to test our limits, to grow, and ultimately to thrive in the face of adversity. It reminds us that despite our vulnerabilities, we possess an inherent strength and resilience that define the very essence of what it means to be alive.

Let the vast, untamed wilderness not be a barrier, but rather a call to adventure—a beckoning to all who seek to know themselves more deeply and to live fully in each moment. With preparation, awareness, and respect for our own limitations and the forces of nature, we are all capable of answering that call.

Chapter 11:
Advanced First Aid Techniques

In diving deeper into the heart of wilderness survival, we've now ventured into a realm where knowledge becomes power, and skills become lifesavers. Advanced First Aid Techniques are the elite tools in your repertoire, designed to confront the gravest of emergencies with confidence and competence. Imagine standing in the wilderness, miles from civilization, and it's your actions, underpinned by your training and courage, that could mean the difference between life and despair. This chapter unfolds the intricate details of Performing CPR, a profound skill that pulses at the core of emergency response. Here, we break down the rhythm of life-saving compressions and breaths with precision, empowering you to sustain a heartbeat against the odds. Transitioning seamlessly, we delve into the science and simplicity behind Using an Automated External Defibrillator (AED), an innovation that brings a jolt of hope in critical situations. Understanding its operation and respecting its power can turn bystanders into heroes.

The wilderness does not distinguish between the seasoned explorer and the novice adventurer; it speaks a universal language that demands respect, preparation, and the willingness to act. Embarking on this journey through Advanced First Aid Techniques, we're not just learning procedures; we're embracing a mindset that sees challenges as opportunities for growth and adversity as a call to rise above. Each paragraph in this chapter is a step closer to becoming the person who doesn't falter when faced with the unimaginable, who can stand firm in the tempest and wield the knowledge that saves lives. It's about channeling your inner strength, guided by wisdom, to make a profound difference in the most extreme of circumstances. Let this knowledge be your companion in the wild, where every decision is a testament to your commitment to safeguarding life, be it yours or another's. With every page turned and every skill acquired, you're not just preparing for the wilderness; you're transcending the ordinary, ready to face the unknown with a heart full of courage and hands equipped to heal.

Performing CPR

In the heart of wilderness, where every second counts and help may be hours away, knowing how to perform Cardiopulmonary Resuscitation (CPR) becomes more than a skill—it transforms into a beacon of hope. Firstly, assess the situation; ensure the scene is safe, and if the victim is unresponsive, call out firmly and check for breathing. If there's no response and no breathing or only gasping, it's time to act swiftly. Place the victim flat on their back on a firm surface. Kneel beside them and place the heel of one hand in the center of their chest, placing your other hand on top. Press down hard and fast, allowing the chest to rebound completely between compressions, aiming for a rate of 100 to 120 compressions per minute. Remember, deep, forceful compressions are crucial—they can be the difference between life and death. If you're trained in rescue breaths and feel confident, alternate 30 compressions with two breaths. However, if you're not, or can't do so safely, continue hands-only CPR. The wilderness demands resilience and readiness; performing CPR effectively is a testament to both. Your actions could preserve a life, offering a fighting chance when faced with the raw uncertainties of nature. Embrace this responsibility with vigilance and courage. CPR is more than a procedure; it's a symbol of hope and human resilience. Remember, in the wild, being prepared to give CPR is not just a skill—it's a duty to those we adventure with and an ode to the sanctity of life itself.

Guidelines and Steps: Performing CPR

In the heart-stopping moments where life hangs in the balance, the knowledge and skills to perform Cardiopulmonary Resuscitation (CPR) can be the difference between life and death. For wilderness explorers and adventurers, mastering CPR is not just a skill—it's a responsibility. The wild offers no easy access to medical facilities, making your action crucial in saving a life. This guide walks you through the critical steps and guidelines to perform CPR in the wilderness setting efficiently.

Understanding the basics of CPR is your starting point. CPR involves chest compressions and rescue breaths, aiming to mimic the heartbeat and breathing until professional help arrives or the heart starts beating on its own. This dual-action process ensures the flow of oxygenated blood to the brain and vital organs, reducing the risk of severe brain damage or death.

Recognizing when CPR is needed is the first critical step. Unresponsiveness and absence of breathing, or only gasping, are telltale signs that CPR may be necessary. It's essential to act swiftly—time is of the essence when it comes to cardiac arrest.

Before diving into CPR, always ensure you're in a safe location to perform it. In the wilderness, this could mean moving the victim away from water, fire, or dangerous terrain. Your safety is paramount; attempting CPR in a hazardous location may lead to two victims instead of one.

Once safety is assured, and you've determined CPR is needed, call for help. If you're in a group, delegate someone to signal or find assistance while you focus on CPR. In remote areas, where signals or help might not be readily available, it's vital to start CPR immediately after ensuring no responsive emergency services can be reached.

To perform CPR, start with hard and fast chest compressions. Position yourself over the victim, with one hand over the other, and press down on the center of the chest. The compressions should be at least two inches deep, at a rate of 100 to 120 compressions per minute. Remember, the song 'Stayin' Alive' by the Bee Gees has the perfect beat for CPR compressions.

After 30 compressions, provide two rescue breaths if you're trained and comfortable doing so. Tilt the victim's head back slightly, lift the chin, pinch the nose shut, and make a complete seal over their mouth with yours. Blow in for about one second, enough to make the chest rise, before continuing compressions.

If you're alone and unable to perform breaths, or uncomfortable doing so, stick with continuous chest compressions. Recent studies show that hands-only CPR can still be effective in adult victims of cardiac arrest.

Utilize resources around you if you're fatigued. In a group scenario, having multiple people trained in CPR can allow you to switch out every few minutes without stopping chest compressions. Continuation without undue delay is crucial until professional help takes over.

Understand that CPR in a wilderness setting may require modifications. For instance, hard surfaces are ideal for performing CPR; however, in the wilderness, you might find yourself on uneven terrain. If a hard surface isn't available, do your best to compress firmly and consistently. Your determination can still make an impactful difference.

It's important to navigate the emotional and physical toll performing CPR can have. While it's physically demanding, the psychological impact of being in a high-stress, life-or-death situation can be substantial. Prepare yourself mentally for these scenarios by practicing mindfulness, stress management techniques, and, if possible, realistic training exercises. Your mental resilience will be as crucial as your physical actions.

Remember, CPR certification and regular refresher courses are invaluable. They equip you with the latest techniques and knowledge, as guidelines may change. Becoming certified through recognized organizations ensures you're prepared to act confidently and competently.

In the aftermath of performing CPR, it's essential to seek support for yourself as well. You may have just undergone a highly stressful experience, whether successful or otherwise. Debriefing with professionals, discussing with peers, or seeking counseling can help manage any emotional aftermath.

Carrying out CPR in the wilderness underscores a powerful act of hope and determination to save a life. While the environment presents unique challenges, your courage to act, informed by these guidelines and steps, encapsulates the spirit of a wilderness adventurer—who, when faced with the trials of nature, responds with resilience, strength, and the profound will to make a difference.

Let each practice, each piece of knowledge you acquire, not just prepare you for emergencies, but also inspire you to embrace the beauty and unpredictability of the wilderness with confidence and peace of mind. Your actions, in those critical moments, echo the profound connection and responsibility we share towards one another, reinforcing the essence of humanity's will to survive and thrive, against all odds.

Using an Automated External Defibrillator (AED)

In the heart-pounding moments of a cardiac emergency in the wilderness, the ability to act swiftly with an Automated External Defibrillator (AED) can turn an outdoor enthusiast into a lifesaver. Understanding its operation and safety nuances is not just about knowing what buttons to press; it's a call to empower yourself with the knowledge that could save a life. When you find yourself in a remote setting, where every second counts, deploying an AED with confidence is crucial. This device is designed to guide even those with minimal training through the process with visual and audio cues, making it a vital piece of equipment in any first aid kit. Remember, before you use an AED, ensure that the person is in a safe, dry area to prevent accidental injury. Following the device's instructions precisely, attach the pads correctly while making sure no one is touching the person during the analysis or shock delivery phases. It's a testament to the marvels of modern technology that even in the backcountry, far from the nearest medical facility, you have the power to make a profound difference. The use of an AED is a critical skill that bridges the gap between immediate response and professional medical care, reinforcing the notion that with the right tools and knowledge, you can face emergencies with courage and determination.

Operation and Safety

When it comes to utilizing an Automated External Defibrillator (AED) in the wilderness, understanding the operation and ensuring safety are paramount. The use of an AED in remote locations presents unique challenges but knowing how to navigate these can mean the difference between life and death. Let's journey through the steps and protocols that ensure the effective and safe use of an AED, as this knowledge can transform you into a beacon of hope in the wild.

First and foremost, familiarize yourself with the AED device before embarking on your adventure. Each model may have slightly different operating procedures, but all are designed with simplicity in mind. A basic understanding includes recognizing the on/off switch, the location of the electrode pads, and where the voice or visual prompts are displayed.

Upon encountering a situation where CPR is being performed, and an AED is available, the first step is to turn on the device. This will launch the automated prompts that guide you through the process. These instructions are designed to be clear and straightforward, eliminating guesswork.

One crucial aspect of AED operation in the wilderness is ensuring the patient's chest is dry and free from excessive hair. Water or sweat can conduct electricity, creating a risk of shock to the rescuer or others in contact with the patient. If necessary, quickly dry the chest area with a cloth and use the razor, if available in the AED kit, to shave any excessive chest hair.

Applying the electrode pads correctly is key. One pad should be placed on the right side of the chest, just below the collarbone, while the other goes on the lower left side of the chest. Ensuring good skin contact without overlap of the pads is essential for an effective shock delivery.

Once the pads are in place, everyone should stand clear of the patient. The AED will analyze the heart rhythm and determine if a shock is necessary. If a shock is advised, ensure that no one is touching the patient or in contact with any water or conductive surfaces connected to the patient. Then, press the shock button when prompted.

After delivering a shock, it's important to immediately resume CPR, following the device's prompts for the correct rhythm and depth of compressions. Continued CPR is crucial until emergency responders arrive or the patient shows signs of life, such as moving voluntarily or breathing normally.

Remember, your safety is also crucial. Avoid using an AED in wet or highly metallic environments to reduce the risk of unintended electrical conduction. Always check the immediate area for puddles, standing water, or metal surfaces that could conduct electricity before proceeding.

The efficiency of an AED in emergency situations greatly depends on the battery and electrode pads being within their expiration dates. Before departing on your trip, verify these components are current and that the device performs a self-check without indicating any fault.

Cultural sensitivity and respect for individual dignity should also guide the use of an AED. Whenever possible, provide privacy or a covering for the patient when exposing the chest to apply electrode pads. Enlist the help of fellow travelers or group members to maintain the patient's modesty.

It's vital to be aware of your jurisdiction's Good Samaritan laws, understanding that these laws exist to protect rescuers who act in good faith and within the scope of their knowledge. Your decision to act could save a life, and these laws generally support non-professional rescuers in emergency situations.

Carrying an AED in the wilderness may seem like an extra burden, but consider it an invaluable part of your first aid kit. Like a parachute in flight, it's better to have it and not need it than to need it and not have it. Let this mindset inspire your preparation.

Learning to use an AED with confidence is not merely about mastering a device, it's about empowering yourself to be a leader in crises, making informed decisions, and performing life-saving acts with competence and courage.

Participation in wilderness first aid and CPR courses that include AED training is an excellent way to develop these skills. Practical, hands-on experience under the guidance of professionals increases your proficiency and confidence in emergency medical responses.

In summary, the operation of an AED in the wilderness demands preparation, understanding, and respect for the profound responsibility it entails. It's about more than following steps; it's about being a vital link in the chain of survival. You have the power to make a difference, to change outcomes, and to save lives. Carry this knowledge and readiness as proudly as you carry your pack, for within you lies the heart of a true wilderness explorer.

Chapter 12:
Mental Health and Crisis Management

In the wilderness, where the unpredictability of nature meets the human instinct for survival, mental health and crisis management become as vital as any physical first aid practice. Venturing into the unknown, equipped with skills to manage not just the body, but also the mind, can be the difference between flourishing and floundering. This chapter delves into the essential strategies for dealing with panic and anxiety, two formidable barriers to clear thinking and effective decision-making in crises. It's about understanding that, while the body may be prepared to endure, the mind must also be fortified. We'll explore practical techniques to calm frayed nerves and provide support, not just for oneself but also for others who might be struggling. Additionally, the specter of PTSD (Post-Traumatic Stress Disorder) in survival situations cannot be overlooked. Recognizing the signs and knowing how to address them can help in preventing a temporary emergency from causing long-lasting psychological scars. By equipping ourselves with knowledge on managing mental health challenges, we do more than survive; we emerge stronger, resilient, and more connected to our fellow adventurers and the natural world around us.

Dealing with Panic and Anxiety

In the unpredictable embrace of the wilderness, where every whisper of wind might signal a new challenge, managing mental health becomes as crucial as tending to physical wounds. Panic and anxiety are natural responses to the stressors of outdoor emergencies; they are your body's alarm system signaling danger. However, in the heart of the wild, mastering the art of calming the mind and steadying the heart becomes a lifesaver. Techniques to mitigate such tensions include deep-breathing exercises, mindfulness, and positive visualization. Deep breathing aids in regulating the fight-or-flight response, providing a moment of pause in the midst of chaos. Mindfulness grounds you in the present, away from the what-ifs that anxiety breeds. Positive visualization, on the other hand, fosters a sense of control and hope, guiding the mind toward constructive outcomes. Remember, courage is not the absence of fear, but the triumph over it. By incorporating these techniques, adventurers and outdoor professionals can cultivate a resilience that not only steadies the nerves but also inspires confidence in the midst of crisis. This chapter arms you with the knowledge to transform panic and anxiety from overwhelming foes into manageable challenges, ensuring your mental health is bolstered to face the uncertainties of the wilderness.

Techniques for Calming and Support

During wilderness emergencies, anxiety and panic can escalate, transforming an already demanding situation into one that's even more challenging to manage. As outdoor enthusiasts, adventurers, and professionals in remote settings, it's crucial to master not only the physical aspect of first aid but also the psychological support techniques that can bring calm to chaos. Beyond the primary goal of safeguarding physical health, ensuring the emotional and psychological well-being of those involved in wilderness emergencies is equally vital.

Maintaining a composed demeanor and leveraging calming techniques are foundational skills in emergency situations. The initiation of a calm presence can significantly influence the emotional state of the casualty, helping to reduce their anxiety and pain and prevent the escalation of shock. It's about creating a bubble of safety and reassurance amidst the unpredictable elements of the wild.

Communication plays a pivotal role in calming someone in distress. Using a calm, firm, and compassionate tone can convey a sense of control and reassurance. It's important to speak clearly and maintain eye contact, which helps in establishing trust. Letting the individual know that help is on the way and that they're not alone in facing their ordeal can be incredibly reassuring.

Listening is just as critical as speaking. Often, individuals in distress need to voice their fears and concerns. By actively listening, you're validating their feelings, which is a powerful tool in calming a panicked individual. This doesn't mean you have to have all the answers; sometimes, just being a thoughtful listener can make a huge difference.

Deep breathing exercises are a practical tool for managing panic and anxiety. Encouraging the injured or stressed individual to take slow, deep breaths can help lower anxiety levels and improve oxygenation, which is especially beneficial if they're experiencing symptoms of shock or hyperventilation. Guiding them through the process by breathing with them can enhance the effectiveness of this technique.

Distraction can be a beneficial strategy as well. Engaging the individual in a conversation unrelated to the current crisis can help shift their focus away from their pain or anxiety. Sharing stories, asking questions about their interests, or simply discussing the environment can redirect their thoughts and help stabilize their emotions.

Physical comfort, when appropriate, can also play a significant role in calming someone. A gentle touch on the shoulder or holding a hand, if consent is given, can be powerful gestures of support and reassurance. These small acts convey a sense of compassion and solidarity.

It's also essential to manage your own emotions and stress levels. The ability to remain calm and composed is contagious; if you're panicked, the person you're trying to help will likely sense your distress and become even more agitated. Practicing mindfulness and being aware of your own emotional state can help you maintain a calming influence over others.

Creating a sense of control over the situation can significantly impact the individual's psychological state. This involves explaining the steps you're taking to help them and reassuring them about the outcomes. Knowing what to expect can help mitigate fear of the unknown, which is a common source of anxiety in emergency situations.

Humor, used judiciously, can be another tool in your calming arsenal. A light-hearted comment can sometimes break the tension and provide a moment of relief. Of course, this must be used with sensitivity to the situation and the individual's feelings.

Visualization techniques can offer a mental escape from the current predicament. Encourage the individual to imagine a place where they feel safe, peaceful, or happy. This mental diversion can reduce stress hormones and shift the focus away from panic or pain.

In cases where individuals are exhibiting signs of severe anxiety or panic attacks, it's important to address their immediate physical comfort. Ensuring they are sitting or lying in a secure and comfortable position can prevent injury and aid in calming efforts. Additionally, maintaining a cool environment, if possible, can help alleviate discomfort and promote a calming atmosphere.

It's crucial to recognize the signs of severe emotional distress, such as uncontrollable crying, hyperventilation, or disorientation. These symptoms can necessitate more focused calming techniques and, in some cases, immediate professional psychological support once out of the wilderness.

Empathy and validation are powerful tools. Acknowledging the individual's experience without judgment can foster a connection and encourage them to focus on calming and coping strategies. Phrases like "It's understandable to feel scared right now" can validate their feelings and encourage resilience.

In summary, the ability to calm and support individuals in distress during wilderness emergencies is a lifesaving skill that complements physical first aid techniques. Through effective communication, empathy, and practical calming strategies, you can help stabilize emotions, reduce panic, and significantly improve the outcome of emergency situations. Remember, in the wilderness, your ability to provide emotional first aid is just as critical as your proficiency in physical first aid procedures.

Recognizing and Addressing PTSD in Survival Situations

In the rugged expanse of the great outdoors, where the unpredictable can become reality, the resilience of the human spirit is often tested. Among the myriad challenges one might face, the specter of post-traumatic stress disorder (PTSD) looms as a silent adversary, its origins rooted in the intensity of life-threatening experiences. Recognizing and addressing PTSD in survival situations is pivotal, not only for the individual's immediate well-being but for their long-term recovery. It's crucial to understand that PTSD might not present itself until well after the danger has passed. Its symptoms—flashbacks, severe anxiety, and uncontrollable thoughts about the event—can gnaw at the very fabric of one's mental fortitude. Encouraging open dialogue about these experiences, providing a supportive ear without forcing the disclosure, and knowing when professional help is necessary, are the cornerstones of addressing PTSD in wilderness settings. Even as we traverse the untamed wild, equipped with the knowledge to sustain our physical well-being, it's essential to remember that our mental health is just as crucial. In the vast uncertainty of the wilderness, where each step forward is a testament to human resilience, understanding and compassion for those battling PTSD becomes a beacon of hope and a testament to our collective strength.

Support Strategies

As we delve deeper into the challenges of wilderness first aid, it's crucial to acknowledge the significance of mental health, particularly in survival situations. One aspect that often goes overlooked is the immediate and long-term psychological support for individuals experiencing severe stress or trauma. This section aims to equip you with the knowledge and strategies necessary to provide this crucial aspect of care.

First and foremost, understand that everyone reacts differently to stress and trauma. What might manifest as panic in one individual could appear as withdrawal or silence in another. Recognizing these variations is the first step in providing effective support. Acknowledgement and validation of their feelings can be incredibly soothing and serve as a foundational step in the support process.

Effective communication is key. This means actively listening to the individual's concerns without judgment. Sometimes, just being heard can significantly reduce a person's anxiety and stress levels. Ensure that your responses are empathetic and supportive, focusing on their feelings rather than immediately offering solutions or dismissals of their fears.

Establish a sense of safety. In wilderness settings, this may mean securing a physical location that is sheltered from the elements or threats. However, emotional safety is equally crucial. Reinforce the idea that they are not alone and that you are there to help them through this ordeal.

Encourage but do not force the expression of emotions. Some individuals may need to talk about their experience, while others might not be ready. Respect each person's pacing and methods of coping. For those who choose to share, listen attentively and validate their feelings.

Help individuals focus on what they can control. In situations of chaos or when feeling overwhelmed, directing attention to small, manageable tasks can empower someone and reduce feelings of helplessness. This could be as simple as setting up a campsite, preparing a meal, or planning the next steps in a journey.

Introduce grounding techniques. For someone undergoing a panic attack or extreme anxiety, grounding exercises can prove invaluable. Techniques such as deep breathing, identifying objects around them, or simple sensory tasks can help bring their focus back to the present and away from overwhelming thoughts or stimuli.

When dealing with potential PTSD or severe stress reactions, be patient and avoid pushing for details or discussions about the traumatic event unless the individual initiates it. Forced recollection can exacerbate stress and potentially deepen the trauma.

Maintain a routine or structure as much as possible. In wilderness contexts, establishing a daily routine can lend a sense of normalcy and security amidst uncertainty. This includes regular meal times, rest periods, and simple group activities.

It's important to recognize when professional help is needed. While providing support in the field is crucial, some individuals may require mental health intervention from a professional. Awareness and acceptance of this limitation are vital, and facilitating access to such help upon return to civilization should be a priority.

In group scenarios, promote a culture of support and openness. Encourage members to look out for each other and to voice their concerns or needs. This collective effort can significantly enhance individual and group resilience.

Stay informed about the signs of more severe mental health issues such as severe depression, persistent anxiety, or PTSD. Early recognition of these signs can ensure timely intervention and support.

Incorporate stress-relief activities. Whenever possible, engage in or facilitate activities known to reduce stress, such as mild exercise, meditation, or even simple games. The goal is to momentarily divert attention from the stressors and allow for mental recovery.

Finally, practice self-care. The ability to provide support to others significantly depends on your own mental and emotional well-being. Adhering to the principles of self-care ensures that you remain capable and prepared to assist those in need.

By integrating these strategies into your wilderness excursions, you not only prepare yourself to handle physical emergencies but also to navigate the complex terrain of mental health crises. Remember, your role as a supporter can make a profound difference in someone's recovery journey, illuminating their path back from distress towards hope and resilience.

Chapter 13:
Legal and Ethical Considerations

As you step into the role of a rescuer in the wilderness, navigating the complexities of legal and ethical considerations becomes paramount. This chapter delves deep into understanding your legal obligations under the Good Samaritan laws, designed to protect those who offer aid in emergency situations from liability. But, it's not just about legality. The essence of wilderness first aid transcends the confines of law; it's anchored in the ethical imperative to make split-second decisions that could mean life or death. Here, you'll explore the moral dilemmas you may face, from deciding who receives care first in a multi-casualty incident to the respectful management of cultural differences in emergency scenarios. This chapter doesn't just inform; it challenges you to reflect deeply on the core values that guide your actions when far from help. As you turn these pages, prepare to engage with scenarios that test your principles, pushing you to harmonize your legal knowledge with the ethical standards that define the essence of humanity in the throes of wilderness adversity.

Understanding Your Legal Obligations

In the throes of wilderness and the unpredictable cloak of nature, every person who steps into the wild shoulders a mantle of responsibility—not just for themselves but for those they encounter. When emergencies arise, and quick action becomes the thin line between peril and safety, it's imperative to understand your legal obligations. The wilderness does not operate within the neat boundaries of urban legality, yet it's governed by laws designed to encourage helping hands without the looming fear of legal repercussions. Good Samaritan laws exist as a beacon of guidance, encouraging every adventurer to extend emergency care with a shield of legal protection, provided the help is offered in good faith and within the bounds of one's knowledge and abilities. This isn't about embarking on a hero's quest fraught with legal pitfalls; it's about knowing that when you act to save a life or alleviate suffering, the law stands with you, not against you. Therefore, understanding these obligations isn't just a chapter in your preparation—it's an armor and a duty, empowering you to make decisions that can mean the difference between despair and hope, between being a bystander and a lifesaver.

Good Samaritan Laws

As we venture deeper into the wilderness, where nature's beauty is matched only by its unpredictability, it's crucial that we not only prepare ourselves with the skills and knowledge to face emergencies but also understand the legal landscape that governs our actions during such events. Good Samaritan Laws play a vital role in this context, providing legal protection to those who offer assistance in times of crisis. These laws are designed to encourage bystanders to lend aid without fear of legal repercussions, fostering an environment where the immediate response to emergencies can often mean the difference between life and death.

In the heart of wilderness, far from the immediate reach of professional medical services, the actions taken by fellow adventurers, hikers, or even casual campers in the critical moments following an accident or health emergency can be life-saving. Good Samaritan Laws vary from state to state, but they share a common principle: to offer legal protection to those who act in good faith to assist others in distress, provided the assistance is voluntary and without the expectation of compensation.

Understanding these laws is essential for anyone stepping into the wild. When faced with an emergency, the willingness to help should not be dampened by the fear of legal consequences should the outcome be less than favorable. This is the spirit that Good Samaritan Laws aim to encapsulate – a spirit of compassion, action, and community support in the face of adversity.

However, it's important to recognize the boundaries set by these laws. They generally do not cover individuals who act recklessly or with gross negligence. The protection is meant for those who perform basic first aid and lifesaving measures to the best of their abilities and within the bounds of their knowledge. This encourages outdoor enthusiasts to get trained in wilderness first aid, ensuring that their well-intentioned efforts are both effective and legally sound.

For those venturing into nature's domain, possessing first aid knowledge and skills becomes not just a personal asset but a communal responsibility. The wilderness does not discriminate, and emergencies can strike the most experienced of adventurers. In such moments, the values of courage, swift action, and empathy are paramount. Good Samaritan Laws support these values by ensuring that the fear of legal retribution does not hesitate a potential lifesaver.

Taking a wilderness first aid course can empower you not just with the skills but also with the confidence to act when needed. It's about being prepared to extend a helping hand, knowing that the law has your back. In many ways, these laws embody the very essence of wilderness ethics: to respect, protect, and support life in all its forms.

Let's also consider the moral aspect of these laws. Beyond the legal protections they offer, Good Samaritan Laws echo a deeper call to our shared humanity. They remind us that in the vastness of the wild, we are at our strongest when we look out for each other. The essence of wilderness first aid is not just about the techniques and procedures; it's about cultivating a mindset of readiness to support and elevate those around us in their time of need.

However, with this understanding must also come a discernment of one's limitations. The ethics of intervention taught in wilderness first aid emphasize the importance of not exceeding your knowledge or abilities. The aim is not to replace professional medical help but to bridge the crucial gap until such help is available. Good Samaritan Laws recognize this delicate balance, providing a safety net that encourages prudent and well-meaning assistance.

In integrating the principles of Good Samaritan Laws into your wilderness adventures, you not only safeguard your legal wellbeing but also reinforce the fabric of mutual aid that is so critical in remote environments. It's about making informed decisions, acting within the scope of your training, and always prioritizing the well-being of those you're assisting.

As we strive to become competent first responders in the wilderness, let us also champion the cause of awareness and education regarding Good Samaritan Laws. Promoting understanding of these laws among the outdoor community enhances the readiness to respond to emergencies with confidence and legal assurance.

In conclusion, Good Samaritan Laws are a fundamental aspect of wilderness first aid that support and encourage the altruistic spirit of helping others in distress. They reflect a societal acknowledgment of the importance of compassion and prompt action in emergency situations. As adventurers, campers, and lovers of the great outdoors, it's essential that we familiarize ourselves with these laws, understand their implications, and carry forward the torch of responsible, informed, and legally protected intervention in times of need.

Let this knowledge empower you rather than burden you. In the wilderness, your actions can make all the difference. Embrace the responsibility with wisdom and courage, knowing that Good Samaritan Laws are there to support you in your pursuit of preserving life. The greatest adventures are those that not only challenge us but also inspire us to be guardians of one another. In this shared journey, let's be ready to answer the call for help with competence, confidence, and a deep respect for the law and the preciousness of life.

Armed with this understanding, we realize that being prepared for the wilderness isn't just about packing the right gear or mastering survival skills. It's also about carrying the knowledge of how to act legally and ethically in the service of others. This comprehensive approach to wilderness readiness not only enhances our own outdoor experiences but contributes to a safer, more responsive outdoor community where everyone can thrive.

Ethical Dilemmas in Wilderness First Aid

In the wilderness, where the rulebook can seem as vast as the landscapes we explore, ethical dilemmas stand as towering peaks and challenging terrains that test the core of our moral compass. At the heart of wilderness first aid lies a web of decisions—each with its own moral and ethical implications that can weigh heavily on even the most experienced adventurers. As we tread these unmarked paths, the question isn't just about what care can be given, but also what should be given, considering the conditions, resources, and the potential outcomes. Deciding whether to continue with a planned adventure or divert precious time and resources to care for an injured fellow trekker can pit the spirit of exploration against the innate human duty to assist. This is the crux of ethical dilemmas in wilderness first aid: navigating the fine line between risk and responsibility, between pushing forward and stepping back. Just as the wilderness demands respect for its power and unpredictability, it also calls for a deep reverence for the sanctity of life and the bonds that form when individuals face adversity together. In these moments, the right decision may not be clear-cut, but with a foundation of ethical guidelines intertwined with the skills and knowledge of wilderness first aid, adventurers are better prepared to make choices that honor both the individual in need and the group as a whole.

Decision Making in Emergency Situations

In the sprawling expanse of the wilderness, where nature commands with absolute authority, the ability to make timely and effective decisions during emergencies becomes a quintessential skill. The serene beauty of the great outdoors can quickly transform into a challenging arena of survival and resilience. This section delves into the heart of ethical dilemmas and critical decision-making processes in emergency situations that one might face in the untamed wild.

The wilderness does not wait for anyone, nor does it slow down. Emergencies in such environments demand swift action and clear-headedness. Making decisions in these high-stake moments can mean the difference between life and death. Whether you're a seasoned explorer or venturing into the wild for the first time, understanding the dynamics of ethical decision-making is pivotal.

First and foremost, the primary goal in any emergency situation is to ensure the safety and well-being of yourself and others involved. This might seem straightforward, but when faced with limited resources, challenging terrain, and the potential for significant harm, the decision-making process can become clouded with complexity.

Consider the scenario where you're hiking with a group and one member sustains a serious injury. The immediate decisions you make—whether to move the individual, how to administer first aid, and determining if and when to leave the injured to seek help—are fraught with ethical considerations. The right choice often hinges on the specific circumstances and requires a balance between immediate action and careful thought.

Effective decision-making in such scenarios is underpinned by a solid understanding of wilderness first aid principles and techniques. It's not merely about knowing what to do, but understanding the why behind each action. This knowledge empowers you to make informed decisions that can greatly improve the outcomes for all involved.

However, knowledge alone is not enough. The wilderness often presents scenarios that textbooks and first aid courses can't fully prepare you for. Here, experience and intuition play critical roles. It's about being adaptable, making the best use of available resources, and sometimes, making hard choices for the greater good.

Another key aspect of decision-making in emergency situations is the ability to stay calm under pressure. Panic and anxiety can cloud judgment and lead to poor decisions. Developing strategies to manage your emotional response and maintain clarity of thought is as crucial as any physical first aid skill.

Communication also plays a pivotal role. In group settings, ensuring that everyone is informed, and their perspectives considered, can aid in making more comprehensive decisions. Yet, in the heat of the moment, strong leadership is required to make final calls and take action.

In addition to immediate emergency response decisions, longer-term considerations also come into play. For example, assessing the potential risks of continuing versus turning back, or deciding whether to split the group. These decisions require not just a understanding of the current situation but also an anticipation of future challenges and consequences.

The ethics of decision-making in wilderness first aid extend beyond the immediate group. Considerations about the environmental impact of your decisions and actions, respect for local wildlife, and adherence to the principles of Leave No Trace are also crucial. Every action taken should be weighed with a sense of responsibility towards the natural world.

Practicing scenario-based training before embarking on wilderness adventures can greatly enhance one's ability to make effective decisions. Such exercises can simulate the stress and unpredictability of real emergencies, providing valuable experience without the actual risk.

Moreover, fostering a mindset of resilience and mental toughness is instrumental. The wilderness, in all its majestic beauty, is indifferent to human struggles. Embracing this fact helps in preparing mentally for the harsh realities one might face and in developing the fortitude to make tough decisions when they matter most.

Ultimately, the art of decision-making in emergency situations is about marrying knowledge with intuition, balancing risk with caution, and leading with conviction. It's about making the best possible choice, with limited information, in scenarios where every second counts.

Remember, the wilderness does not provide easy answers. Every situation is unique, each decision critical. In the end, the best one can do is to prepare diligently, act with purpose, and learn from each experience. The path through the wilderness of uncertainty is paved with the stones of courage, wisdom, and the will to make the right decisions, even when faced with the toughest dilemmas.

As you venture into the great outdoors, carry with you not just your survival kit, but also a steadfast commitment to making informed, ethical decisions. These choices not only define your experiences but also ensure that the wilderness remains a place of awe-inspiring experiences for generations to come. Embrace this responsibility with a fervent heart, for in the realm of the wild, your decisions carve the path forward—not just for you, but for all who tread these untamed lands after you.

Well-Being Publishing

This Book Review Request

In embarking on this journey through the wilderness of first aid and emergency care, it's crucial to understand that your thoughts and experiences can light the way for others; sharing your review of this book is not just appreciated, it's an act of extending a hand to fellow adventurers, ensuring that together, we stride confidently into nature's embrace, better prepared and more connected.

Conclusion

Embarking on a journey into the wilderness brings a sense of freedom, adventure, and connection to the natural world that is both invigorating and humbling. It reminds us of our place within the larger ecosystem and the responsibility we carry not just for our safety but for those we journey with, and the environment itself. Through this book, we've ventured together into the essential skills, knowledge, and attitudes necessary for managing emergencies in remote settings. As we close this chapter, let's consolidate our learning and reflect on moving forward.

Wilderness first aid is not merely about treating injuries or illnesses in isolation; it's a comprehensive approach to prevention, preparation, and response that requires foresight, presence of mind, and a commitment to ongoing learning. The skills you've been introduced to are foundations upon which to build further expertise. Just as nature is dynamic, so too should our abilities to adapt and respond to whatever challenges it may present.

Remember, preparing a wilderness first aid kit is an essential step, not just for what you pack in it, but also for the thought process and understanding that goes into its compilation. Each item selected is a testament to the anticipation and preparation for the unexpected. This mindset of preparedness is what can often make the difference between a minor mishap and a serious emergency.

The principles of emergency management emphasize that in a crisis, your greatest asset is your ability to stay calm, assess the situation clearly, and take decisive action. Training and preparation can condition your response, but it's your mindset that will guide you through the turmoil. Nurturing a calm, positive, and proactive mindset is just as critical as mastering technical skills.

Engaging with the environment, whether through hiking, camping, or professional work, carries with it an inherent responsibility to respect and protect it. As you've learned to navigate through and respond to environmental hazards, let that knowledge extend to practicing and promoting sustainable and respectful outdoor ethics. It's about leaving no trace, preserving what we have so that future generations can enjoy and learn from it too.

Dealing with bites, stings, and wildlife encounters are vivid reminders of the wild's unpredictability. But they also teach us respect and caution, reinforcing the importance of coexisting with the myriad other forms of life that call these places home. It's a poignant reminder of the balance within ecosystems, and the interdependence of species, including our own.

Wound care, managing bleeding, and addressing shock are fundamental skills not just for wilderness settings but for life. They instill a confidence in being able to help, to make a difference when it counts. This confidence, however, should always be tempered with humility and the awareness that nature's forces are far greater than ourselves.

Sprains, fractures, water safety, and drowning prevention are areas where knowledge can truly save lives. They underscore the vital importance of risk assessment and making informed decisions. Sometimes, the bravest thing we can do is to decide not to proceed, to turn back, or to seek another path. Courage in the wilderness is as much about knowing when to forge ahead as it is about knowing when to retreat.

In navigating common health issues, dealing with allergies, and managing chronic conditions, we're reminded of the incredible adaptability and resilience of the human body. We're also reminded of the need for empathy, understanding, and support for those we're with, who may be facing their own unique challenges in these settings.

The advanced first aid techniques, including CPR and the use of an AED, are critical skills that could mean the difference between life and death. They represent a pinnacle of first aid training, where the actions of a single individual can give someone the most precious gift of all: a second chance at life.

Addressing mental health and crisis management, we begin to understand that sometimes the most profound wounds are not those that bleed. Awareness, compassion, and the ability to offer support are invaluable in helping ourselves and others through difficult times. It's a powerful reminder that first aid extends beyond the physical.

Legal and ethical considerations touch upon the moral fabric that holds our society together. They call on us to not only do what's legally right but what's morally commendable. In the wilderness, where we are often at our most vulnerable, these principles can guide our actions towards doing the greatest good.

As we conclude, it's important to remember that what you've learned is only the beginning. The journey of education is lifelong, and each experience in the wild is an opportunity to grow, to learn, and to become more adept in our skills. Whether you're a seasoned adventurer or someone who dreams of venturing into the great outdoors, let this knowledge empower you. Let it be a catalyst for exploration, for pushing boundaries, and for discovering the indomitable spirit within each of us.

May the trails you walk be safe, may your journeys be rewarding, and may the wilderness continue to inspire, challenge, and enrich your life. Here's to your adventures in the great outdoors, armed with knowledge, preparation, and a respect for the natural world. Let's step forward with confidence, responsibility, and a heartfelt commitment to safeguard ourselves, our fellow adventurers, and the environment we treasure.

In the embrace of the wild, may you find both the serenity of solitude and the camaraderie of shared challenges. May your spirit be fortified by every sunlit path and starlit night. And remember, the greatest adventures are not just those that take you to new vistas but those that bring you closer to understanding yourself and the intricate, beautiful tapestry of life on this planet. Onward, to your next adventure, with wisdom, courage, and a compassionate heart.

Appendix A:
Appendix

In the journey through wilderness first aid and emergency preparedness, we've explored the importance of knowledge, preparation, and action. As you step into nature's vast playground, remember that the real world is the ultimate classroom. Here, in Appendix A, we provide you with tools designed not just to complement the chapters you've journeyed through but to serve as a tangible bridge between the knowledge you've gained and its practical application.

Wilderness First Aid Checklist

Being prepared is more than a motto; it's a vital component of outdoor safety and adventure. A well-assembled first aid kit is your first line of defense in managing unexpected situations. Think of it as your best friend in the wild—a friend you hope not to need but one you're grateful to have when the unexpected occurs. Consider this checklist as a starting point, adaptable to your expertise, the nature of your adventure, and the environment you'll be embracing.

- Comprehensive first aid manual
- Assorted adhesive bandages
- Sterile gauze pads and adhesive tape
- Antiseptic wipes and antibiotic ointment
- Over-the-counter pain relievers

- Prescription medications if required
- Blister care and prevention items
- Tweezers and scissors
- Thermal blanket for managing shock or cold
- Splinting materials

This list is not exhaustive but serves as a foundation upon which to build, depending on personal needs and trip specifics.

Emergency Communication Planning

Communication is your lifeline in scenarios where immediate help is required. Modern technology offers a plethora of tools designed to break the silence barrier when off the grid. The key here is preparation. Before venturing out:

1. Inform someone about your plan, location, and expected return.
2. Research and understand the area's emergency frequencies or contact numbers.
3. Carry a charged cell phone and a portable backup charger.
4. Consider investing in a satellite communicator or a personal locator beacon for remote adventures.

Having a communication plan is not only a beacon for you but provides peace of mind for those who care about you.

Recommended Reading and Resources

Knowledge is power, and in the context of wilderness first aid, it's a lifeline. The learning doesn't stop here; it's a continuous process. Here are some resources that come highly recommended:

- **Wilderness Medicine** by Paul S. Auerbach: A comprehensive guide that offers in-depth information on a vast array of wilderness medical situations.
- **The Wilderness First Aid Handbook** by Grant S. Lipman: Practical, concise, and easy to understand, this handbook is perfect for quick reference in the field.
- **Survival Skills of the North American Indians** by Peter Goodchild: Though not a first aid book, understanding survival skills can be crucial in managing emergencies.

Additionally, consider taking hands-on wilderness first aid courses offered by reputable organizations such as the American Red Cross or Wilderness Medical Associates. There's no substitute for practical, hands-on experience under the guidance of professionals.

As you turn the pages of this guide and those recommended here, remember that each step you take into the wilderness is a step towards understanding and respecting the untamed nature of the great outdoors. Your preparation, knowledge, and courage are what make those steps safe and rewarding.

Equip yourself, embark on your adventures, but above all, embrace the journey with respect, preparation, and a continuous thirst for learning. The wilderness awaits.

Wilderness First Aid Checklist

Stepping into the wilderness requires not just courage but preparation. It's a truth universally acknowledged by seasoned adventurers and novices alike: the wilderness doesn't distinguish between the two. As we've journeyed through the essentials of wilderness first aid and emergency techniques, it's clear that knowledge is power, but it's also just the beginning. Equipped with this power, the next step is physical preparation - assembling a first aid kit that isn't just a box of supplies, but a beacon of safety and reassurance in the vast unknown.

Imagine you're miles from the nearest road, surrounded by the untouched beauty of nature, and an accident happens. It's not just about having band-aids or antiseptic wipes; it's about having a well-thought-out collection of items that can effectively handle the situation until professional help is available. This wilderness first aid checklist is tailored for outdoor enthusiasts, designed to address a vast array of potential scenarios, from minor injuries to life-threatening emergencies.

Foremost, your first aid kit should include personal protective equipment (PPE) like gloves and face shields. Safety first – not only for the injured but for the rescuer. Infections and diseases can spread even in the wildest of places, and your health is as crucial as the person you're caring for.

For wound management, ensure you have sterile gauze pads, adhesive bandages of various sizes, antiseptic wipes, and antibiotic ointment. Cleanliness is next to godliness, especially when it comes to treating open wounds in environments where cleanliness is a challenge.

Bleeding can turn a minor injury into a major one if not controlled quickly. Include materials such as hemostatic dressings and a tourniquet in your kit. Knowing how to use these can be as essential as the items themselves, so invest time in learning proper application techniques.

Burn relief ointments and sterile dressings should also find a place in your first aid kit. Forests and campsites are filled with fire hazards, and burns, whether from a campfire or sun exposure, need immediate attention to prevent complications.

Fractures and sprains are not uncommon, and having elastic bandages and splints can provide the necessary support to stabilize the injury. Additionally, including a cold pack for inflammation can be a game-changer in reducing pain and swelling.

Insect bites and stings can turn from a minor irritation to a significant threat if left untreated, especially in areas prone to mosquitoes and ticks. Pack treatments for bites and stings, as well as a tick removal tool. Remember, prevention is key, so also consider insect repellent as a first line of defense.

Medications play a vital role in a first aid kit. Pain relievers, antihistamines for allergic reactions, and any personal medications should be in ample supply. Adjust quantities based on the length of your trip and the number of people in your group.

Dehydration and water purification methods must be included. Hydration salts or tablets can make the difference in preventing dehydration, a common yet dangerous risk in the wild. A portable water filter or purification tablets ensure that you always have access to clean water.

Don't forget the tools that can make first aid administration easier: tweezers for splinters, a medical thermometer, scissors for cutting cloth and bandages, and a comprehensive first aid manual. Knowledge in your head is invaluable, but having a reference can help under stress.

A flashlight or headlamp is another critical addition. Many emergencies happen at night, and visibility is paramount to assessing and addressing injuries effectively. Ensure it's durable and waterproof, tailored for the unpredictability of wilderness conditions.

Communication devices, although not technically part of a first aid kit, cannot be overlooked. A satellite phone, a whistle, or a mirror for signaling can be lifesavers, literally, when it comes to getting help in remote areas.

Last but not least, customize your kit based on the environment you'll be exploring. Specific risks associated with different terrains or weather conditions may require additional items. Whether it's a high-altitude sickness medication or ice packs for hotter climates, tailor your kit to fit your adventure.

As you gather each item, remember that this checklist is more than just a list; it's a testament to your commitment to safety and preparedness in the face of nature's unpredictability. With each piece of gear, you're not just packing; you're planning for success, ready to face whatever challenges come your way with resilience and resourcefulness.

The journey through the wilderness is as much about exploring the external landscapes as it is about understanding the depths of our inner strength. Your first aid kit, meticulously prepared and packed, becomes a symbol of this journey. It represents foresight, responsibility, and the profound respect for nature's power. It equips you not just with tools, but with confidence, ensuring that you're ready to enjoy the wilderness safely, securely, and sustainably.

Emergency Communication Planning

In the realm of wilderness adventures, where the unknown meets the unprepared, the thread of safety weaves through the fabric of proper communication planning. Venturing into the great outdoors isn't just about escaping the daily grind; it's a journey that demands respect for nature's grandeur and unpredictability. Thus, embedding efficient emergency communication planning into your adventure narrative isn't optional—it's essential.

Understanding the landscape of your adventure is your starting point. Different terrains—whether desolate deserts, dense forests, or towering mountains—pose unique challenges and necessitate specific communication strategies. Knowing the terrain's challenges can inform your choice of communication tools, whether it's satellite phones, personal locator beacons (PLBs), or two-way radios. It's not merely about having a device; it's about knowing the ins and outs of your chosen communication lifeline.

Before you set out, make a comprehensive plan. This should include detailed route information, expected check-in times, and clear instructions on what to do if those check-ins are missed. Share this plan with someone trustworthy who's not part of the trip—consider this person your safety anchor. They should have a clear understanding of your timeline and be prepared to initiate help if your check-ins become echoes of silence.

The digital age has equipped us with various tools and apps designed to bolster our safety net in the wilderness. Apps that track your location and share it with designated contacts can be lifesavers. The harnessing of technology to ensure safety cannot be overstated; however, it's vital not to become complacent. Batteries die, and gadgets malfunction, especially in harsh environmental conditions. Hence, backup physical maps and compasses must never be deemed obsolete. Understanding how to navigate the traditional way remains an invaluable skill in emergency situations.

Communication isn't just about relaying a cry for help; it's also about preempting potential threats. Weather apps and emergency alert systems can keep you one step ahead of nature's fickleness. Staying informed can mean the difference between a minor adjustment in plans and a full-blown crisis.

In instances where communication technology fails, knowledge of traditional signaling methods becomes paramount. Three of anything (blasts of a whistle, flashes of light, fires, etc.) universally signify a call for help. Learning and practicing these signals before embarking on your journey can empower you in times of dire need.

One often overlooked aspect of emergency communication is the psychological comfort it can provide. Knowing there's a way to reach out, to bridge the gap between isolation and connection, can bolster spirits and ignite a beacon of hope in grim situations. This mental boost is not trivial; in survival scenarios, hope and morale are as critical as any physical tool.

The integration of a PLB or a satellite messenger in your gear can be a game-changer. These devices have one primary function: ensuring your SOS message makes it out, with precise location details, thereby drastically reducing search and rescue times. Investing in such technology is investing in your safety and peace of mind.

Training and practice are the undercurrents that give strength to your emergency communication plan. Familiarize yourself with your devices before you need them. Understanding the how-tos in a calm environment builds confidence; in moments of crisis, reflexive knowledge can take over, smoothing the edges of panic.

Community knowledge is an invaluable resource. Engaging with local authorities or experienced adventurers who know the area can provide insights into potential hazards and better prepare you for emergencies. Tailoring your communication plan with local wisdom not only enhances safety but also deepens your connection to the places you explore.

In the tapestry of wilderness adventure, your narrative is intertwined with the unseen and the unforeseen. Adopting a flexible mindset towards emergency communication planning is essential. Conditions change, and with them, your strategies might also need to adapt. Flexibility in the face of the unpredictable can make all the difference.

Remember, the goal of embarking on these wilderness journeys isn't merely to conquer or to survive. It's to harmonize with the environments we explore, to understand and respect the forces of nature, and to return enriched by our experiences. Effective emergency communication planning is an act of respect—towards nature, towards our fellow adventurers, and towards ourselves.

As you pen the chapters of your own adventure story, let emergency communication planning be the ink that ensures the narrative is one of triumph, wisdom, and safe return. After all, the true essence of adventure lies not in escaping life but in ensuring that every journey, no matter how remote, is a return home.

May your adventures be many, your experiences rich, and your communications clear. The wilderness beckons with its untold stories and unseen beauty, but it also commands respect and preparation. Equip yourself with the knowledge, skills, and tools for effective communication. Let the serenity of being prepared provide the backdrop for your wilderness symphony. In the heart of the wild, be connected, be safe, and above all, be ready to embrace the profound transformation that comes with facing the unknown, armed with wisdom and a robust emergency communication plan.

Recommended Reading and Resources

As we explore the final sections of this guide, it's crucial to recognize that learning is a continuous journey, especially in the fields of wilderness first aid and emergency care. The resources and literature provided here are selected to deepen your understanding and enhance your skills beyond the scope of this book. Each recommendation has been carefully picked to cater to the diverse interests and professional requirements of outdoor enthusiasts, campers, hikers, and those working in remote areas.

First on the list is "Wilderness Medicine" by Paul S. Auerbach. This comprehensive text is widely considered the bible of wilderness medicine. It covers a broad range of topics, from basic first aid procedures to managing complex medical emergencies in isolated environments. Auerbach's detailed explanations and practical advice make it an indispensable resource for anyone serious about wilderness health and safety.

"Mountaineering: The Freedom of the Hills" by The Mountaineers Books provides an exhaustive guide to outdoor skills, and although not exclusively focused on first aid, it contains crucial chapters on emergency preparedness and response that are invaluable to adventurers of all kinds. The insights into altitude sickness, frostbite management, and emergency shelter construction are particularly noteworthy.

For those who appreciate learning through real-life scenarios, "Deep Survival: Who Lives, Who Dies, and Why" by Laurence Gonzales, offers riveting accounts of survival against the odds, alongside analysis of what contributes to making effective decisions in critical situations. Gonzales's exploration into the psychology of survival complements the more technical aspects of wilderness first aid beautifully.

The National Outdoor Leadership School's "NOLS Wilderness Medicine" offers robust guidelines and instruction, designed not just for reading but for practical application. Its emphasis on prevention and decision-making processes under duress are standout features that equip readers with the mindset needed for outdoor emergencies.

For a more compact resource, "A Field Guide to Wilderness Medicine" by Paul S. Auerbach, Howard J. Donner, and Eric A. Weiss is perfect for on-the-go reference. It distills key information from the larger tome of wilderness medicine into a portable, easy-to-navigate guide, making it an excellent companion on any excursion.

Understanding the legalities and ethics of providing first aid in remote locations is also crucial. "Wilderness and Rescue Medicine" by Jeffrey Isaac, PA-C, and David Johnson, MD, covers these topics in depth, ensuring that caregivers not only provide medical help effectively but also navigate the complexities of consent and liability.

In the digital age, online resources are invaluable. Websites such as Wilderness Medical Society, Red Cross, and Centers for Disease Control and Prevention offer up-to-date information on wilderness first aid protocols, training programs, and health alerts that can inform your practices and keep your knowledge current.

Interactive learning through online courses can also supplement your hands-on training. Platforms like Coursera and Udemy feature courses on wilderness first aid, basic life support, and emergency medicine fundamentals, often taught by seasoned professionals in the field.

Don't underestimate the power of local workshops and training programs, either. Organizations such as the American Heart Association and National Outdoor Leadership School offer nationwide courses in CPR, AED use, and wilderness first aid that provide practical, hands-on experience under the guidance of experts.

Podcasts on outdoor safety, survival skills, and wilderness medicine are great for those who prefer audio learning. They can be surprisingly enlightening, offering tips, stories, and interviews with experts in the field. Look for reputable series that focus on medical preparedness and outdoor adventures.

Community engagement, through forums and social media groups focused on wilderness medicine and outdoor adventures, can also be a treasure trove of information. These platforms allow for the exchange of ideas, personal experiences, and advice that can broaden your understanding of wilderness first aid.

Books on mental health and crisis management, such as "The Unthinkable: Who Survives When Disaster Strikes - and Why" by Amanda Ripley, can offer insights into the psychological aspect of survival and emergency response. Understanding the human element in crises can significantly affect the success of your interventions in wilderness settings.

Finally, it's worth noting that the journey to becoming proficient in wilderness first aid and emergency care is both challenging and rewarding. It requires dedication, practice, and continuous learning. The resources listed here are starters, meant to ignite your passion and guide you through the next steps in your education.

As you continue to explore, experiment, and engage with the wilderness, keep in mind that your knowledge and skills can make a significant difference, not only in your own adventures but also in the lives of those around you. Stay curious, be prepared, and keep learning. The wilderness awaits, and now you're better equipped to face its challenges with confidence and competence.

www.ingramcontent.com/pod-product-compliance
Lightning Source LLC
Chambersburg PA
CBHW031156020426
42333CB00013B/686